the Unauthorized TEACHER'S SURVIVAL GUIDE

second edition

AN ESSENTIAL REFERENCE FOR BOTH NEW AND EXPERIENCED EDUCATORS!

BY JACK WARNER AND CLYDE BRYAN, WITH DIANE WARNER

Park Avenue

The Unauthorized Teacher's Survival Guide, Second Edition

© 2001 by Jack Warner and Clyde Bryan, with Diane Warner

Published by Park Avenue, an imprint of JIST Publishing, Inc.
8902 Otis Avenue
Indianapolis, IN 46216-1033
Phone: 1-800-648-JIST   Fax: 1-800-JIST-FAX   E-Mail: editorial@jist.com

Visit our Web site at **www.jist.com** for information on JIST, free job search information, book chapters, and ordering information on our many products!

> Quantity discounts are available for JIST books.
> Please call our Sales Department
> at 1-800-648-5478 for a free catalog and more information.

Acquisitions and Development Editor: Lori Cates
Cover Designer: Katy Bodenmiller
Interior Designer: Aleata Howard
Page Layout Technician: Carolyn J. Newland
Proofreader: David Faust
Indexer: Tina Trettin

Printed in the United States of America
05 04 03 02 01   9 8 7 6 5 4 3 2 1

Library of Congress Cataloging-in-Publication data is on file with the Library of Congress.

We have been careful to provide accurate information in this book, but it is possible that errors and omissions have been introduced. Please consider this in making any career plans or other important decisions. Trust your own judgment above all else and in all things.

Trademarks: All brand names and product names used in this book are trade names, service marks, trademarks, or registered trademarks of their respective owners.

ISBN 1-57112-110-2

Dedication

With love to our children, grandchildren,
and all those yet to come.

Acknowledgments

W e want to thank our editor for the first edition, Sara Hall, for without her encouragement and support, this book would have never been written. Our thanks also to Lori Cates, Development and Acquisitions Editor, who supervised the updated second edition.

We also want to thank all those educators who participated in our survey, especially those on the staffs of Osborne School, Julien School, Crowell School, Campus Park School, and Ceres Unified School District. Special thanks to Dave Sutton, Zelma Corbin, and Claudia Matthys, who so generously helped with the monumental task of distributing and retrieving teacher questionnaires. We want to thank Holly Myers for her help with Web site research and Karlee Myers for her help updating the second edition. Extra-special thanks to Beth, our cheerleader, whose enthusiastic help and support kept us going throughout the research and writing of this book.

About This Book

The mission of this book is to save you years of trial-and-error so that you'll not only "survive," but "thrive," in your teaching career.

Whether you're a first-year teacher or an experienced old-timer, we offer practical, user-friendly advice to help prevent teacher burnout. You'll learn how to fit in with the staff at your school, establish rapport with your students and their parents, handle discipline problems, and manage the stress of teaching.

You'll also learn inside secrets of managing your time, juggling a teacher's many hats, and coping with extracurricular duties. Other nitty-gritty issues are covered as well, including how to prepare for a substitute and create a positive classroom environment.

We think teaching is the noblest profession of all and we want you to thrive in your career as a teacher.

Contents

Introduction

Here you are, a teacher with a diploma in one hand and a teaching contract in the other, filled with idealistic expectations. After a few days on the job, however, the smile fades, the rosy glow turns to ashen gray, and your gut tightens as you encounter the "real world" of education. Whether you are a new teacher or an experienced one facing a new assignment, your job can seem overwhelming at first.

"They never told me it would be like this," cries the neophyte.

"This new situation is so different from my last," comments the old-timer facing a different school district and new grade level.

Your student-teaching experience may have gone well, with help from your master teacher. The small class seemed controllable with its bright, cooperative students. But your student teaching didn't prepare you for your real-life class of 34 students, many with learning and behavioral problems. "Why do these kids seem so big?" you whisper to yourself.

A diploma and teaching certificate entitle you to be called "teacher," but it takes many years of experience to actually become a teacher. Teaching is an honorable and rewarding profession, and it should be fun. For many of us, however, the job isn't much fun at first because of the overwhelming responsibilities. Teaching is a job that never seems to get "done." The custodians finish their daily routine and wave as they drive out of the parking lot; their duties are done until tomorrow. Ah, but the teacher's day is much different.

Here is a typical scenario for the kind of day you may be having: At the end of the teaching day, when you're physically and mentally exhausted and your desk is a mass of papers, you still need to attend a staff meeting. Finally, you pick up your daughter at child care, stop by the grocery store to buy Pampers and milk, help prepare dinner, and clean up the kitchen. Then you bathe the baby and get her off to bed. By this time, it's 8 o'clock, the "perfect" time of day to grade papers and write in details for tomorrow's lesson plans.

You struggle to pull your brain together long enough to finish these plans, being distracted, meanwhile, by a movie on television in the next room. Your "significant other" stares at the TV all alone, again.

The day's crises flash through your mind: "I should have known Timothy would throw up. I should have sent him to the nurse's office right after lunch. I should have had a project ready for Jennifer and Jason—they always seem to finish the reading lesson too soon. I should have noticed that Jimmy and Mario were playing way too rough during recess and that someone would get hurt...." So many "should have's."

Then there are all your questions:

- "How will I ever fit in with the staff?"
- "What do they expect from me?"
- "How do I handle 'problem' parents?"
- "What should I be doing about the field trip next week?"
- "How do I prepare for the parent conferences?"
- "How much time do teachers usually spend in preparation? Why does it seem to take me so long?"
- "What happened to my home life? Will I ever be able to relax and enjoy my family in the evening?"
- "Do I dare ask my aide to watch the class if I need to handle a student's behavior?"
- "How can I cope?"
- "How do I stay organized?"

- "What should I do if I think one of my students has head lice? Can I get it, too? What if I bring it home to the family?"

- "How do I order videos for science? Is there a special form to fill out?"

- "What if I get sick? Who do I call? How will I prepare lesson plans in time for a 'sub'?"

- "How do I lighten up and keep a little humor in the day?"

If these questions sound familiar, we're here to help. Although it usually takes years of experience, mostly trial-and-error, to finally feel in control, we want to share our 50-plus years of experience with you so that you can feel confident from the start.

Many teachers never do reach this level of confidence and self-esteem because they give up too soon. This is known as "teacher burnout." The overload of responsibilities, so common in our country, becomes overwhelming. The teacher is required to wear many hats: Substitute Parent, Social Worker, Reading Specialist, Nurse, Playground Supervisor, Family Counselor, Disciplinarian, and more. In many other countries, the teacher is required to wear only one hat: Teacher. In this country, however, your hat rack is full. In the chapters that follow, we will help you juggle your hats and find humor in it as well.

We want you to be proud of your profession even though the rewards of teaching may not be immediately apparent. The fact is, however, that you can have a positive impact on the lives of the students entrusted to you each year, the proof of which may not show up until they are grown adults.

Guy Dowd, recent national Teacher of the Year, offers pertinent perspectives on the teaching profession. He asks the question "Which teacher impressed you the most when you were in school? The one who taught you the most facts? Or the one who made you feel good about yourself, who had your best interest at heart?"

Mr. Dowd feels that as a teacher you are one of the greatest sources of influence on a child's life. He feels the teacher's role is a sacred one and that we should truly care for each student, building his or her self-esteem.

If we all care as much for our students as Guy Dowd does, we will realize that we who have chosen the teaching profession are in a marathon, not a sprint. The influence you have on a student's life will mold him as an adult. What an opportunity we have as teachers in our society! What a rewarding profession we have chosen!

Remember that the impressions you make in your students' lives, much like a computer virus, may lay dormant for many years, surfacing in their adulthood. Don't ever feel guilty at the end of a teaching day, thinking you have failed. If you made a difference in one child's life that day, you were a success!

Our goal in this book is to help you feel comfortable and confident as a teacher. Whether you are embarking on your very first year of teaching or you're an experienced teacher who is still struggling with the complexities of the teaching life, we want to encourage you. We want you to learn to pace yourself for the long haul, realizing that each teaching day is a success in itself.

Your college professors have prepared you for your teaching career by giving you a solid background in theory, methods, and applications, and you got a taste of the real world in your student-teaching experience. This book picks up where your college training left off by offering practical ways to deal with the countless nonacademic aspects of the teaching profession.

There is an old saying that "A wise man benefits from experience, but a wiser man benefits from the experiences of others." Our goal is to help "tutor the teacher" by answering your questions, relieving your doubts, and replacing your frustrations with confidence.

Keep your sense of humor and remember: Teaching is a marathon and *not* a sprint!

Part I

Preparing Yourself for Teaching

Chapter 1

Fitting In
with the Staff

Your first classroom is something special—it's the place where you and a group of youngsters you have yet to meet will share the next school year.

There are several important things you can do ahead of time that will help you fit in and feel comfortable once school starts. First, familiarize yourself with the community, school policies, your students, your school, and the buzz words peculiar to the profession. Next, meet and begin to build relationships with the school's staff—not only your fellow teachers, but every other member of the staff as well.

Five Ways to Jump-Start Your Year

While you await the key to this kingdom, you can be doing five constructive things to give yourself a head start on your year.

Become Familiar with the Community

First, become familiar with the community as a whole. Take in lunch at one of the local restaurants; attend a Little League game. Observe all the community activities you can work in and meet some of the locals while you're at it. Your feel for the community will become invaluable as you establish rapport with your students, their parents, and the staff of your new campus.

Read Up on Policy

Next, get hold of policy handbooks for the school district and for your school in particular. Once you're caught up in staff meetings and classroom preparation, you may never find the time to study these policies in detail, and you should be familiar with them from the start.

Read Up on Your Students

The third thing you can do is examine the cumulative folders of your students, which should be available in the school office. When you read through these folders, do so with an open mind. They will probably contain such things as family background, who to contact in case of emergency, personal characteristics and social skills, peer relationships, comments from past teachers, health records, and test scores.

Try not to prejudge any child because of these test scores. In our years of teaching, we have often found that a student will achieve higher than previous test scores would indicate. Some teachers deliberately avoid these scores, in fact, to prevent any prejudgments. Also, you should very carefully weigh any comments you find in the cumulative folder regarding past behavior because a child's behavior can vary from year to year.

One thing you should examine closely, however, is each student's health record. Look for references to unique health problems, such as vision or hearing problems, allergies, and so forth.

Become Familiar with the School

The fourth thing you can do is become familiar with the school's physical layout. Locate everyone's office, the supply room, the teachers' workroom, the cafeteria, the nurse's office, the library, and the administrative offices. Be sure to locate all the restrooms available for students, as well as those designated for teachers.

Become Familiar with the "Buzz Words"

Finally, if you really want to get a head start on your year, become familiar with the buzz words. We have provided a user-friendly glossary at the back of this book that contains terms and acronyms peculiar to the teaching profession. Study these buzz words until they become second nature to you. That way, you'll feel more comfortable when veteran teachers toss them around over lunch or in the teacher's lounge.

Your New Coworkers

Now that you have killed as much time as you can stand, the day finally arrives when you are issued "The Key." The frustration at this point is that you will probably gain access to your classroom about the time staff meetings and orientation sessions begin. You will long to escape to your room, but will need to focus on these meetings and fitting in with the staff.

The following sections give you some suggestions on how you can begin relationships with your new coworkers. You will learn what each of the staff members can do for you and, likewise, what you can do for them. Let's begin with your fellow teachers.

The Teaching Staff

The first people you will meet are the other new teachers. They may be new to the teaching profession, or they may be experienced teachers new to this school or district. New-teacher staff and orientation

"Make friends before you need them."

meetings begin a day or two before the regular staff is required to report. These meetings will be the only time all new teachers get together as a group. You will feel a bond as you share stories of your common struggles to get through school and find a job. You will all have the same apprehensions and questions regarding your upcoming teaching year. These new-teacher staff meetings can be invigorating and encouraging.

The first general staff meeting of the year may be more intimidating than the new-teacher meetings. You will be inundated with names, which you will vainly try to implant in your brain. Unless you're a Dale Carnegie graduate and have mastered the art of name association, however, you'll be lucky to remember the names of your principal and two or three teachers. Try to see the humor in all of this—relax and enjoy the camaraderie and the names will come in time. First, try to memorize the names of all the teachers at your grade level. After you've done that, set a goal to learn two or three names a day before the first day of school.

As you're getting to know the other teachers on staff, look for the "friendly faces." These are the teachers who will sincerely offer help, and every school has some. You will be able to tell who these people are from the very first meeting. Some individuals just have a helping and giving spirit; if you sense this about certain teachers—and you will—take them up on their generosity and learn their names right away.

Those of us who have had many years in the teaching profession all seem to agree that the three staff members you should befriend first are the secretary, the custodian, and the cook, for good reasons you will discover later in this chapter. Let's just say it's smart to learn their names quickly.

By this time, you will know whether you have been assigned to some sort of team, either as part of a team-teaching partnership or because of the proximity of your classrooms. There may be four of you, for example, in one "pod" (a grouping of classrooms), whose rooms all open into a common room that can be used for storage, supplies, audiovisual equipment, TV, VCR, computers, work tables, and so on. Meet your team members and find out when the first team or grade-level meetings are scheduled and what is expected of you at these meetings.

Here's another way to fit in quickly with the staff: Make sure that you're clear on your duty assignments, especially regarding playground, bus, detention, lunch room and recess duty, and chaperoning. Most schools don't assign duty to new teachers during the first week of school so that they will have a chance to locate the duty roster and familiarize themselves with expectations.

When you are assigned to playground duty, it's a good idea to chat with another teacher on duty. Learn the school's playground policies, especially regarding boundaries. Also, it is a good idea to find out exactly when and where the buses load and unload and where your students should line up after school.

Chaperoning duties for events like school dances are usually divided up evenly over the school year and the teachers are scheduled at the beginning of the year. The same policy holds true for football, basketball, and other sports events. Unfortunately, it's a sad fact that our society has come to the point that many school districts hire security guards to take this duty, and often the games themselves are held at a neutral site to avoid problems.

Remember the friendly faces we mentioned earlier? These teachers will answer your questions regarding duty assignments, and it's a good idea to tag along with them whenever you can. In any case, when it comes to your duty assignments, be punctual, cheerful, and cooperative. This will help you fit in with the staff.

You should also try your best to fit in socially. As a new teacher on staff, you may feel intimidated by all the names and commotion and want as much quiet time in the classroom as possible. Although the feeling is understandable, fight it. Otherwise, you might slip into the "hibernation habit." A good example of this is a new teacher at one school who ate lunch at her desk while reading a novel. It bored her to chitchat with the others over lunch. She also avoided the faculty lounge. As a result, this habit deprived the teacher of an opportunity to meet fellow staff members, share ideas with them, and become a member of the team.

Here are some tips to help you fit in socially:

- Eat lunch with the other teachers as often as possible (no matter how painful it is to be away from your desk).

- Contribute financially to any "kitty" the other teachers may have going. Usually there are funds collected to buy flowers for someone in the hospital or for birthday or new-baby gifts. Don't participate grudgingly; at least fake a cheerful attitude and always make the contributions as soon as they are requested.

- Make friends with your teachers' association representative. You will eventually need to decide how active you want to be in this association, but it's a good idea, especially your first year in the district, to at least act interested in what the association is doing. Attend a few of their meetings and get to know your local school rep, because that person is knowledgeable about the issues. Also, the other teachers will notice your interest.

One word of caution regarding your fellow teachers: Beware of teachers with negative attitudes. You'll know who they are right away. These negative staff members will be clouds of gloom; you'll need an umbrella when you're around them because they'll rain all over you. If you listen to these "downer" people, your morale will drop to the basement as they complain about the students, their rooms, the administrators, the system, the school board, the small pay raise, the bad cafeteria food, the local vandals who break into schools, and anything else they can dump on you. The old-timers on staff have been avoiding these resident iconoclasts for years; but you, as a newcomer, have fresh ears. Recognize that there are negative people in all professions, but teaching is difficult enough without this type of negativism. So, seek out those friendly faces who care about you and who have positive attitudes.

The Principal

Every principal has a different personality. Some encourage friendly, impromptu chats, while others maintain a distance between themselves and the staff. It all depends on the person's administrative style. One principal may want to stay close to the staff, being aware of what is going on in every classroom. This type will tend to drop in and casually interact with the teacher and students. Other principals leave the classrooms up to the teachers and become involved only at the teacher's request or when a formal evaluation has been scheduled.

When you come on staff in a new school, assess your principal's style as soon as possible. Don't walk into your principal's office and plop down for a visit unless you're sure you will be welcome. The best advice is to use common sense. Talk to your teaching team or grade-level cohorts to get a feel for the communication level between the principal and staff.

One policy you can probably count on, however, is that until you learn differently, assume that you are responsible for handling most discipline problems. The principal could handle them for you, but it's important and more effective for you to learn to handle them on your own. A good rule of thumb is this: "Don't have a hair trigger." In other words, don't refer students to the principal for minor problems, such as chewing gum. Wait for something major, such as a student who has left the playground to walk to town, for example. Your school probably has a written discipline policy that defines exactly when a problem becomes serious enough to warrant referral to your principal.

The Vice Principal

Not all schools have an administrator who bears this official title. Many smaller schools have no one in this position; larger schools may have a long-term staff member who fulfills these duties. If your school has a vice principal, this is probably the administrator who handles discipline problems referred from teachers.

The School Secretary

Here is a person some consider to be one of the most important members on staff. A good secretary can hold things together and keep the school running smoothly, even when the principal and vice principal are not on campus. Usually the secretary is more accessible than either administrator, and it's important to establish excellent rapport with this person.

Here are a few of the hundreds of things he or she will do for you:

- Answer your school-related questions.

- Keep you informed of meetings and school activities.

- Handle the paperwork for your sick leave.

- Arrange for a substitute.

- Handle emergencies (call the ambulance, call parents, and so on).

- Set up special meetings between teachers and parents.

- Take your messages.

Here are some of the things you can do for your school secretaries:

- Do everything they request in a timely fashion.

- Don't burden them with your personal problems.

- Don't expect them to take more than a reasonable number of personal messages. (Don't have friends and family call you at school if they can call you at home.)

- Don't expect them to take care of your nonschool business. (A teacher at one school was so brazen as to run his side business out of the school office. He even had the school telephone number printed on his business cards as his office number.)

- Unless told otherwise, don't ever use the secretaries' office equipment. (You will have a teachers' workroom that furnishes a computer, copy machine, laminator, and so on.)

- *Remember National Secretary's Day!* Do something to show you appreciate the secretarial staff on this special day. In fact, have your students write thank-you notes for all that the secretaries do.

- It doesn't hurt to remember your secretaries with thank-you notes, thoughtful flowers, or boxes of candy through-out the year as well. The key is to stay on the good side of your school secretaries because they are valuable staff members.

The Custodian

Here is another important staff member. Custodians frequently fall into the category of "lovable characters," and it is common for them to play Santa at Christmas or dress up at Halloween. The successful custodian is often popular with the kids, who beg for little jobs they can do to help. Everyone in the teaching profession agrees on one thing: Good custodians don't get paid nearly what they're worth.

Here are a few of the things the custodians will do for you:

Before the school year begins:

- Find extra furniture for your classroom.
- Move heavy classroom furniture.
- Find extra desks for your students.
- Make repairs to your room.

Throughout the school year:

- Adjust the height of desks as needed.
- Clean your room.

- Empty your trash.
- Clean your chalkboards and erasers.
- Retrieve playground balls off the roof.
- Etc., etc.

What you and your students can do for the custodial crew:

- Place chairs on desks on certain designated cleaning days.
- Avoid using colored chalk, if requested.
- Clean up any clay or broken crayons that have stuck to the carpet, floor, or desks.
- Pick up any staples or straight pins that drop onto the carpet (they won't vacuum up).
- Don't use Scotch tape on chalkboards or any painted or varnished surfaces.
- Keep hanging plants out of custodians' pathways when they are cleaning your room.
- Get rid of anything that stinks, such as rotten food, smelly pet litter, science materials, and so on.
- Have your students help out by emptying pencil sharpeners or banging erasers clean outdoors (not against the sides of any building or on sidewalks because chalk dust won't wash off easily).
- Write *Save* on the chalkboard if you don't want your lesson to be erased.
- Ask before making a major change in your room arrangement. For example, you may ask, "I am planning to arrange the desks in groups of four. Will that be a problem with your vacuuming?" Normally this would never be a problem, but very few teachers think to consult with the custodians ahead of time; those who do are really appreciated.

- Ask what your students can do to make their jobs easier.

- Don't be a complainer! Remember, the entire staff works together as a team and the custodian is to be respected.

- Show the custodians your appreciation throughout the year. Thank-you notes are in order, not only from you, but individual thank-yous written by your students. Once a fourth-grade class made creative thank-yous that were illustrated with drawings of the custodians doing their work. The crew got such a kick out of these drawings that they pinned them up on the walls of their workroom. Very few teachers realize how much a little praise can mean to a custodial staff.

If you treat your custodians with the respect and appreciation they deserve, you will not only make them feel like part of the team; you'll also reap rewards!

The Cafeteria Staff

As we have already mentioned, the cook ranks right up there with the custodian in importance. Members of any kitchen crew usually come with a built-in reputation. Some are gruff and demanding; others are easygoing.

A head cook at one school was known as the "town tyrant." She was mean and grouchy; the whole staff was afraid of her. The goal was to avoid anything that would make her mad, such as lingering over your lunch. She wanted everyone to eat quickly and return their trays immediately so that she could get them washed. We finally figured out that we could eat our lunches in peace if we unloaded our trays onto the tables and returned them before we even began to eat.

You may find some unique characters on your cafeteria staff, and they can be a lot of fun.

Here are some things they can do for you:

- Furnish a hot lunch program.

- Provide teachers' lunches.

- Prepare bag lunches for your students' field trips.
- Help with treats at special events like school programs.

Here are some things they expect from you:

- Have your class lined up for lunch at precisely the correct time.
- Arrange for the collection of students' lunch money.
- Let them know in advance the exact number of bag lunches you'll need for an upcoming field trip.
- Abide by their unique cafeteria rules. Find out what these are by having a chat with a friendly face.
- Speak directly with the head cook to see whether everything is going well with your students. Your concern will pay you dividends at some point in the future.

The Teaching Aides

You are very fortunate if you have been assigned an aide, whether the assignment is full- or part-time. Using the help effectively is important, and that doesn't come easily for a first-year teacher.

One school had a new teacher who was assigned a full-time teaching aide. This should have been good news, but turned out to be a disaster instead. This teacher was so occupied with his own lesson plans that he never took enough time to enlist the help of his aide. His teaching could have been much more effective if he would have assigned certain daily duties to his assistant.

The key is to meet with your aide before the school year begins. Ask questions; determine your aide's strengths and weaknesses. One aide may enjoy designing bulletin boards and displaying students' work, but may feel ill at ease in front of the class. Another may feel comfortable teaching small groups of students. Aides appreciate the respect you show by involving them in your ongoing planning. This gives them a chance to suggest ways they can help achieve your goals.

It's important to remember that classroom aides do not replace you; they assist you. They do not just correct papers, but should also be used for personal interaction with pupils in your classroom.

Teachers should remember to praise and thank their aides throughout the school year, and it doesn't hurt to bring them cards on their birthdays or little gifts at Christmas. They are valuable members of the staff and need to feel that way.

The Resource Teacher

Don't confuse a resource teacher with the person who runs the resource room. The latter is usually called a *media specialist*.

A resource teacher is usually on staff under special funding and works in a pullout program. This type of program is for students with identified learning disabilities who are pulled out of regular classrooms for special help from the resource teacher.

Look at your list of students to see whether any were pulled out in previous years. If so, you will need to determine whether they need pullout time again this year. You also need to find out how many hours per week and what days and times the resource teacher is available.

If you have students who have never been referred to a resource teacher, but may need help now, find out the procedures for referral. Is testing required? Do you need parental permission? Is there an established referral process?

Some schools are funded for several resource teachers; get to know the one available to your students.

The Librarian or Media Specialist

This person is in charge of the school's library or media center, which usually includes books, tapes, periodicals, resource materials, and audiovisual equipment.

Here are the things this specialist can do for you:

- Order or reserve books and materials to be used with your planned teaching units.

- Order audiotapes or videotapes.

- Help familiarize your students with the use of the library.

- Reserve audiovisual equipment, including a television set or VCR.

This is what this specialist expects from you:

- Place all orders or reservations in ample time.

- Schedule your students' library visits according to policy.

If possible, go to the media center before the school year begins to practice using all the audiovisual equipment. It's an even better idea to wheel each to your classroom so that you can try it out in your own environment. If you don't take the time to do this, you are asking Murphy to come for a visit, because anything that can go wrong, will.

Once there was a teacher who was asked to audition for a position that became available during the school year. She was asked to teach a lesson to a class of students while the principal and superintendent observed. Her lesson was going along fine until she tried to use the overhead projector. She positioned her transparency and it was projected onto the screen behind her. She didn't notice until she glanced back that it was upside down. She became flustered and, instead of turning her transparency, she turned the entire projector around, which meant she was now projecting onto the back wall.

The children giggled as she struggled to figure it out. She finally got it all together and finished the lesson. She was hired in spite of this incident, but I'm sure she wishes she would have spent more time with that projector.

The Teaching Specialists

A teaching specialist is someone who is hired to teach your special classes, such as art, music, or physical education. During difficult economic times, these staff members are usually the first to be cut. So if you have them available, be grateful.

The main thing you need to know regarding these specialists is whether you are expected to stay alongside as they teach. In many districts, policy allows teachers to use these periods for prep time. Find out your school's policy regarding "specials." If you are expected to be present during class time, be as cooperative as you can.

Professional Help

Most districts provide certain support personnel who can be called on a case-by-case basis. One of these professionals is a speech therapist, who will help students who have speech disorders or impairments.

Another is a psychologist, who will conduct diagnostic testing or meet with the student, family, teacher, and administrator to work out problems.

A social worker is another type of professional available to school districts and is usually the one called in case of suspected child abuse or neglect. In many states, it is a misdemeanor if suspected abuse goes unreported.

The School Nurse

In most cases, a school may not have a full-time nurse; he or she may be on your campus only certain days and hours.

Here are some of the things the nurse can do for you:

- Maintain student health records.

- Provide you with any life-threatening history noted in your students' records, such as allergy to bee stings, seizures, and so on.

- Administer vision and hearing tests to students.

- Take care of students who become ill during school hours.

- Make home visits.

- May become involved if child abuse is suspected.

- Will contact the student's home in case of illness, communicable disease, or head lice.

Here are some of the things the nurse expects from you:

- Alert him or her to students' vision or hearing problems.

- Refer any students who become ill.

- Refer any students with impetigo, head lice, or other communicable diseases.

- Alert him or her to possible home health problems that may require a home visit.

- Be the nurse's eyes and ears; watch for any health problems your students may have.

By the way, if you ever discover a student with head lice, you'll probably be scratching your scalp the rest of the day!

The School Bus Driver

Introduce yourself to all the bus drivers who may be transporting your students and take extra time to get to know the driver for your class's field trips. You will discover that every bus driver has a different tolerance level. One might want absolute quiet when driving; another may not care whether the bus sounds like a football stadium. Also, some drivers want the teacher to sit up front; others don't care where you sit. If you want to hit it off from the start, ask the driver for his or her preference. Should the kids keep it down to a gentle roar, or should you just keep them from singing "99 Bottles of Beer on the Wall"? And where does the driver want you to sit?

Some of a bus driver's pet peeves are kids who don't let you know when they're going to throw up, kids who sneak food and drink on the bus, and kids who get too rowdy. The bus driver's primary mission is to get passengers to their destination safely.

The School Board

You will make a great impression if you attend board meetings from time to time, and not just when salaries are being discussed. Board members are looking for teachers who are interested in all aspects of running their school district. It's especially important for you to attend the specific board meeting at which you are formally hired. Board members like to meet new employees.

Conclusion

By now, you can see that it takes dozens of people to run a school; you are just one member of the team. Even though you are new on staff, you can become a real team player. Here are two last words of advice when it comes to fitting in with the staff:

- As the year progresses, ask other staff members what you and your students can do to make their jobs easier.

- Show your appreciation during the year with thank-you notes, thoughtful cards or gifts, and even a simple word of praise now and then.

Very few first-timers make this kind of effort. If you do, it will set you apart. You will become known as the new teacher who is cooperative, appreciative, and friendly. By the way, a sense of humor really helps, too.

As the year progresses, you'll find that you're not only fitting in with the staff, but becoming well-liked and a valuable member of the team. Remember—make a friend before you need one!

Chapter 2

Rapport with Your Students

Finally, the fun begins! You've spent four or five years preparing for this moment: The first day of school. After all those late nights of study, grueling exams, and exhausting job interviews, you finally have your very own classroom filled with students whose lives you'll touch this year. After all, if you didn't think you could make a difference, you would have entered some other profession, right? You might have chosen a career in the computer field at twice the income. Or perhaps you toyed with occupations in other lucrative fields—accounting, communications, or business. But you chose to become a teacher, an honorable position that can change lives. And because of this possibility, you will never face a more important task than the one you face now: establishing positive rapport with your students during the first week of school.

This chapter attempts to make your early experiences with your students as comfortable and upbeat as possible by passing on some of the insights we have learned in our years of teaching. We have found that when establishing rapport, you need to know the mechanics, which can be learned, and you need to care, which is a matter of the heart.

The Mechanics

The mechanics include all the things you can do to establish rapport, such as learning students' names, deciding on a seat-

ing chart, and explaining the daily schedule and the class rules. Also, you have control over the personal impression you make:

"Of all the things you wear, a smile is most important."

Your dress, voice, body language, mannerisms, and use of humor all tell students quite a bit about your personality. The paragraphs that follow give you a closer look at these mechanics.

Learning Names

Name tags on desks are usually a good idea at first. Prepare them ahead of time, being careful to spell the names correctly. The students will probably line up at the door of your classroom; you can give them their name tags as they enter. Introduce yourself to each student and be sure to smile! Write your own name on the board so that they can see how it is spelled.

Seating

Some teachers like to arrange the desks in groups of four or five so that they can mix up students with varying cultural and academic backgrounds. Other teachers prefer to let the students select their own seating, making them feel as relaxed and comfortable as possible on the first day of school. In either case, seating can be changed as necessary if the mesh of personalities doesn't work.

Daily Schedule

As part of your preparations for the first day of class, you will have planned a daily schedule, which will include the preliminary rituals, such as saluting the flag, taking the roll and lunch count, and collecting milk money and homework. In addition, the schedule should include the rest of the activities for the day, including each subject, recess, lunchtime, and so on. Make enough copies of this schedule so that, in addition to the one you post in your classroom, each student can have a copy to take home to his or her parents. Go over this schedule with your class on the first day; this will give them a comfortable feeling because they will know what to expect, which is an important factor in building positive rapport from the start.

Class Rules

In addition to the daily schedule, also post a copy of the class rules. Take time to go over these rules with your class, including such things as

- Your lending policy: Never allow students to take or use anything from your desk without permission (Scotch tape, paper clips, and so on). You will quickly discover the value of this rule.

- The restroom policy: Explain which restrooms are for students' use. Encourage them to use the restrooms during lunch or recess and explain your procedure for dismissing them during class.

- The procedure for checking out library books kept in the classroom.

- Your rules for the use of any equipment located in the classroom (audiovisual, cassette player, computer, and so on).

- The procedure for dispensing supplies, such as crayons, paper, paints, pencils, and so on.

- Your policy on students using the drinking fountain.

- The procedure for cleaning up after a project and at the end of the day.

- All the special rules of your school regarding lunches, buses, playground equipment, behavior, and so on.

Obviously, students can follow the rules only if they know what is expected of them. So making the rules clear is an important part of establishing rapport.

Your Dress

You'll hear two extreme differences of opinion when it comes to teachers' attire. The first view is that a teacher should dress up, not down. That is, dress as nicely as possible, wearing professional business attire. Proponents of this extreme feel that we have a certain duty to look like a teacher—to be a role model. These people insist that you'll never have more authority than your dress commands.

The other extreme view is to "dress down" to the level of the students, giving them the impression that you are like them—at least as far as clothes are concerned. Proponents believe that students need to feel you're an "all right" person, and that seeing you in more relaxed clothing helps promote this. Even if you're 40 years old, they say you should wear the clothes of a 15-year-old because you will relate to the students better.

Before making your choice, first ask about the dress code for your district; most school boards have established informal expectations and these are your primary guidelines. Personally, we suggest dressing up or at least taking a middle ground by dressing neatly and appropriately. Dressing down could be a real mistake; students may see through what you're doing and suspect a shallow attempt to get on their good side. As a result, you lose some of your authority (not to mention credibility).

The bottom line is this: In our opinion, your job will be easier if you dress above your students.

Your Voice

One of the most difficult tasks for new teachers is to discipline themselves to keep their voices low and soft. The tendency, obviously, is to increase the volume and raise the pitch of your voice, especially as frustrations build and the students' noise level seems to be getting out of control. The lesson to learn is this one: You cannot out-scream 30 voices. The louder you scream, the louder the classroom becomes. It's a dangerous precedent to set, especially as you establish rapport with your students on the first day. There is no way you'll last out the year if you have to scream all day long—you would have to be carried home in a litter! Keep your voice low and never give way to screaming! How do you get them to quiet down if you can't raise your voice? By using body language.

If you have 30 screaming kids, your problems are more serious than voice level. Voice level can be a factor only if you've established basic classroom management and control from the outset.

Body Language

Here are a few ways to quiet a classroom by using your body language:

- Stop talking, stand very still, and raise a hand. One by one, students will notice, stop talking, stand still, and raise their hands as well. When every student is quiet, resume what you were saying.

- Stop talking, stand very still, and try to make eye contact with the students making the most noise. This works well.

- Continue to speak softly while casually walking over to the worst offender and laying your hand on the student's shoulder. This not only quiets that student, but gets the message across to lesser offenders as well.

Mannerisms

When it comes to personal mannerisms, the worst thing you can do is try to be something you're not. Some teachers believe you should act as stern and unyielding as possible during the first few weeks of school to let the students know you're in control. Then, after six weeks or so, they say you can relax a little, smile more, and ease up on the class. We believe it's never a good idea to force unnatural mannerisms to make a point. The children will see right through you; they will sense that you are faking it, which is a difficult thing to do over a

"Be gentle with the young."
—Juvenal

long period of time, by the way. The answer is to let your natural mannerisms take over: Be yourself. You can set a tone for your classroom, starting the first day of school, without compromising your own personality.

Humor

One of the best lessons you'll learn from this book is this one: Keep humor in your teaching! Here is a concept that doesn't come easily for new teachers, who may feel that too much "silly" and not enough "serious" will cause them to lose control of their classrooms.

Many teachers, experienced ones included, find it difficult to inject humor into each day. But you did, after all, choose a profession that cries for joy and laughter! Just think of those poor souls who decided on a career in accounting or computers—how much laughter fills their days? Teaching, however, lends itself to laughter, or at least it should.

In the beginning, you'll find humor in your students. In fact, you'll fight to keep a straight face as one explains how his homework went through the wash in his jeans pocket or how another came home from school to find a litter of kittens delivered on her pillow by a neighborhood cat. In fact, each student's personality will have its humorous side; this alone should give you 30 chuckles a day. Keep a smile on your face and always be looking for humor in your students.

Your own natural sense of humor, even if it's pretty dry, should be unleashed each day as well. Your students will look forward to your quirky humor, even in the smallest ways. One teacher we know, when starting her class on an activity that is to be timed, occasionally says, "Ready, Set...Wait!" Because she doesn't always say "Wait," the students watch her, smiles on their faces, wondering what she will say this time.

Use humor in your games, too. You can play a simple little game called "Going Camping" on the first day of class to lighten things up and help the students get to know each other at the same time. The game begins with the teacher, who says, "I'm Mrs. Simmons and I brought a tent." The next student in line says, "Mrs. Simmons brought a tent; my name is José and I brought a fishing pole." The next student says, "Mrs. Simmons brought a tent; José brought a fishing pole; my name is Marcie and I brought some worms." Any game that can make the class laugh will work.

Humor comes naturally, as well, to music. (It's a good idea, especially during the first week of school, to involve the kids in group singing.) If you have a guitar or other instrument and can lead the class in singing, it will relax all of you, particularly if you know some humorous songs. There are sing-along tapes that you can use in place of or in addition to your instrumental accompaniment. In the lower grades, the sillier the better. For example, my class loves the song "I Wanna Be a Dog" because of the humorous lyrics. When we come to the line "I wanna have dog breath," we usually find even the shyest students laughing.

Another form of humor is the simple joke; there is definitely a place for it now and then. And a little teasing works well, too, although you should tread lightly at first, getting to know which students like to be teased and which do not.

Humor is essential; it builds rapport easily because the students perceive you to be open and sincere—someone they can relax around and be themselves. Many teachers don't realize that students sometimes come with preconceived opinions. Perhaps they heard through the playground grapevine that you're "mean" or "scary." You want to alleviate any of these misconceptions on the first day, and humor is a perfect tool. You may also want to tack up some humorous photos of you and your family so that your students will see that you are a real person. This is one more way to break down the barriers and establish rapport.

The Caring

The mechanics of establishing rapport seem insignificant compared to the more important mission of showing your students that you care. You will soon discover that your students arrive with all the baggage of their pasts. Although you may not see it in their eyes on the first day of school, many may have been abused or neglected, shunned, teased, or shuffled between parents or other relatives. Many others may have poor self concepts because they don't speak English, are low academic achievers, or come from disadvantaged backgrounds. You will feel more like a counselor or psychologist at times as the school year progresses (we get into that in chapter 5, "The Teacher's Many Hats"). But for now, let's just say that it's important to build your students' self-esteem, and you can do this by showing them that you care, beginning on the first day of school.

You may never master all the mechanics, but, in our opinion, it barely matters as long as you care for your students. This caring, as we mentioned before, comes from the heart and the children can read it easily; they will know from the start whether or not you sincerely care for them. By caring for them, you build their self-esteem, and it begins on the first day of school. The following sections give you insight into some of the best ways to show that you care.

Don't Prejudge Any Student

Assuming that you have studied each child's cumulative folder, you may be tempted to tag certain students with labels, such as "Discipline Problem," "Slow-Learner," "At-Risk Student," and so on. You may also be influenced by comments overheard in the teachers' lounge, such as "You got Jonathan this year? Lots of luck! Boy, do you have your work cut out for you!" If you're new on staff, and especially if you're new to the teaching profession, you may absorb this stuff like a sponge. But from our experience, we can assure you that prejudgments are often unfounded.

Beginning on the first day of school, give all your students a clean slate. Treat each one as an individual who deserves your respect and love. Treat each child with a positive attitude, expecting him or her to achieve, respond, and contribute. Show each child courtesy and treat him or her as you would like to be treated; you'll be surprised to see the difference this will make. These simple philosophies will bring out your students' best and gain their respect, as well.

Guy Dowd, recent national Teacher of the Year, saw such value in each of his students that he actually came to school early, sat at an individual student's desk, and prayed for that student's well-being. Then, as the school day began, he expected to see improvement in that particular student as he looked for ways to praise and show that he cares.

Recent studies have shown that Guy Dowd's philosophy works. Even in cases where the students had no parental support at all, there was higher achievement and improved self-esteem for students whose teachers had positive expectations and who truly cared.

Avoid Sexism

The younger the children, the less aware they are of gender differences; as they grow older, however, this becomes more of a factor. When we first started teaching, back in the early '60s, the boy/girl thing didn't become a problem until about seventh grade. Now, you see it in the third and fourth grades. The older the children, the more important it is to be aware of sex equity.

Never tease a girl, for example, who wants to go out for the football team, and never tease a boy who wants to take cooking lessons. In our own school districts, we have seen several successful role reversals: one girl on our wrestling team and two girls on the football team (one is a placekicker and one is a defensive back).

One trick that will prevent you from accidentally using sexist language is to pluralize words. For example, you could say "the nurses...they" instead of "the nurse...she" or "the airline pilots...they" instead of "the pilot...he." This should keep you out of trouble.

On the other side of the scale, be sensitive to genuine gender differences. For example, girls are more apt to hang onto each other as they walk, want to hold your hand, and "chitchat." Boys, on the other hand, tend to be a little noisier and more active than girls. This energy, by the way, can usually be spent on the playground running or playing a sport.

Respect Your Students' Religious Backgrounds

In the spirit of establishing good rapport with your students, be sure to honor and respect their religious backgrounds. Examine their cumulative folders ahead of time to see whether any of your students have certain prohibitions. For example, if you have any children with Jehovah's Witness backgrounds, be aware that they are not allowed to participate in many holiday celebrations, cannot salute or pledge allegiance to the American flag, and can't sing the national anthem. If you have children with Jewish backgrounds, be sensitive to the fact that they usually do not celebrate Christmas, although they may participate in some of the activities. They do, however, celebrate Hanukkah, which is close to Christmas and can be incorporated into your December plans. You should plan appropriate alternate activities for these students. Sensitivity to your children's religious backgrounds is just another way to show them you care and respect them as individuals.

Respect Your Children's Ethnic and Cultural Backgrounds

Few things are as exciting and enjoyable as a class filled with children from various cultures, and it's important that we instill in our students the respect for each other's backgrounds. Even with our best efforts, however, difficult—although sometimes amusing—incidents occur.

The important thing is to show respect for each child, regardless of background, by encouraging them to share their unique differences with the class as a whole. You can do this in dozens of ways, but here are some of the most popular ideas:

- Celebrate several ethnic holidays, such as Cinco de Mayo or the Chinese New Year.

- Present a dance program in which each ethnic group demonstrates its traditional dances.

- Have an International Food Day, on which each group brings samples of its unique dishes.

- Have a school parade in which the students can show off their costumes.

- Fill your classroom with inviting multicultural books for your students to read.

- Invite parents or members of your community to come into your classroom to talk about their cultures.

- Plan multicultural art projects.

Take photos of all these activities and build an international photo board that displays them alongside a world map that indicates each student's town or country of origin.

Awards, Rewards, and Praise

Think up as many ways as you can to praise your students and to make them feel good about themselves. Here are some good ideas:

- **Student of the Week.** Be sure that each student in your class receives this award at least once during the school year. You may want to include a display of the student's work along with photos you have taken ahead of time. Many children come from homes where their photos are rarely taken, so this is a special "stroke."

- **Student of the Month.** This award is an even bigger honor and usually includes a few very special things, such as a presentation from the school principal at an assembly, a photo of the student receiving the award, a special pizza, and so on.

- **Give the students positive affirmation** by writing special praise at the top of their papers or using praise stickers for their work.

- **Emphasize and praise each student's talent.** If the child can sing, dance, or play a musical instrument, have the student perform in front of the class. If the student writes interesting poetry, have the child read it aloud, and so on. Every child does something well; watch for it and show it off in front of the student's peers.

- **Teach your students a skill** that will give them self-confidence. We have found that chess is good to teach, as is any handcraft, such as fly-tying, cooking, sewing, or woodworking. Certain children will excel in these skills, which provides another opportunity for praise and peer recognition.

- **The Jelly Bean Jar.** You can use something as simple as a jar of jelly beans to help build self-esteem. Give a student some jelly beans as a reward for positive behavior. Be sure this recognition, as small as it seems, is visible to the class.

- **Encourage applause.** Whenever it is appropriate, encourage the class to applaud a student's presentation or performance.

> "Pay attention to the young and make them as good as possible."
>
> —Socrates

Turn the proverbial lemons into lemonade. For example, one teacher noticed that his class had one "odd-ball orphan" desk that was always embarrassing for a student to use. The students avoided it and the one child who got stuck with it was embarrassed. The teacher recognized this problem, so he came in one Saturday and sprayed it with gold paint and decorated it. From that point on, this desk became an esteemed place for the Student of the Week to sit.

Look for ways to praise each student every day. There is something positive you can say to each one. This is so important that you should even keep a list of the students to use as a checklist to be sure that you don't miss one. A student should never leave your classroom at the end of a day without having some form of praise. Another reason for a checklist is to be sure you include the isolates. These are the students who go unnoticed in any group situation: the shy one who seldom makes eye contact; the last to be chosen for a team; the one who seldom, if ever, causes problems; the wallflower at the dance. Studies have shown that these children especially need positive recognition every day. Sit down by yourself several times during the school year and focus on each student individually. Think about each one's needs, aspirations, and self-esteem; what can you say or do that will boost that child's self-image?

Make Your Students Feel Like Part of a Family

You want all your students to feel part of a family, and it's especially important in a multicultural classroom because one of the primary goals in bilingual education is to build self-esteem. Here are some good ways to create a feeling of family between you and your students and among the students themselves:

- **Create a safe environment.** Assure them that you will never hurt or embarrass them in any way; you'll never let them hurt each other, physically or verbally. You want your students to know you will protect them. They must feel comfortable and safe in your classroom, no matter what clothes they wear, how they achieve, or what they say. Each child should be able to say "I know my teacher likes me—I can take a chance in here and not be hurt." This will not come quickly for certain students, particularly those who are shy or have a language barrier. But keep working at it, starting with the first day of school and throughout the year.

- **Get to know your students well.** There are many ways you can get your students to tell about themselves. One way is through biographical writing assignments. Another is by writing in a journal. Ask them to write about their home, family, pets, what they like to do, and so on, and encourage them to ask you questions about yourself. This will open up a dialogue.

- **Help the students get to know each other.** You can have willing students read their biographical writing assignment aloud to the class, present a "show-and-tell" about favorite items from home, or perform in front of the class. Also, all the multicultural activities mentioned earlier can help students get to know and accept each other.

- **Create individual or small-group relationships with your students.** Whenever you can spend time with a child on an individual basis, you will establish rapport and build that child's self-esteem. As a reward, for example, have lunch with a certain student some day. That child will know that instead of eating with the other teachers, you chose to eat lunch with her. (She doesn't need to know that teachers sometimes aren't a lot of fun at lunchtime, anyway, because they tend to talk shop, something you know your students won't do.) You might even want to stay after school and shoot baskets with some of your students, kick a ball, or sit down with a small group and do a science project. You will be seen in a different light; immediately you will go from authoritarian to friend. Keep this rapport within the school boundaries, however; it's not a good idea to extend these relationships to other activities in your personal life.

Whenever appropriate, it's important to give an affectionate pat on the head, a hug, or just a squeeze of the shoulder. Many children don't receive pats and hugs at home, so it's especially important for them to receive them somewhere!

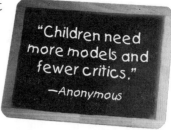

"Children need more models and fewer critics."
—Anonymous

Celebrate each child's birthday. Make as big a deal as you can out of each birthday, including singing, a card from you and the class, and at least a small gift, such as a lollipop or pencil. If you have a bilingual class, you will find cards in various languages for sale at your local teacher supply store. For any birthdays that fall on days when school is not in session, celebrate ahead of time.

Demonstrate Self-Esteem

Be a role model to your students, demonstrating your own self-esteem. Believe in yourself; be confident; be positive; expect the best from yourself each day. Your positive attitude will bring positive response from your students. This will happen naturally and all you need to do is *enjoy your class*.

Conclusion

By establishing and maintaining rapport and high self-esteem among your students, you may even save an at-risk child from his textbook fate. Yes, you have chosen a profession that definitely makes a difference in lives, and this is important for you to remember when you've had a particularly lousy day. Even if your lessons didn't go as planned, you felt out of control, you didn't handle a discipline problem well, or you felt like a failure, if you cared for your students that day, it was a successful day!

Chapter 3

Rapport with the Parents

C hildren are an extension of their families, and so it is important that you get to know the parents and encourage them to join your team. As corny as it may sound, you and the parents are (or should be) working together. For your students to succeed in school, you need the parents on your side. As this chapter explains, there are many ways to win them over.

Opportunities to Meet Parents

Most schools offer four major opportunities for parents and teachers to meet: Back-to-School Night, Open House, parent-teacher conferences, and kindergarten orientations.

Back-to-School Night or Open House

Back-to-School Night is usually held just after the start of the school year. The meeting gives teachers an opportunity to meet parents early and put faces with names. Back-to-School Night is more structured than an Open House. The teacher usually offers an overview of the year's program and suggests ways parents can help with their children's educations. Adult classroom volunteers, such as classroom aides and room parents, are also signed up at this time.

In most schools, Open House usually takes place in the spring. This night gives teachers an opportunity to showcase their students' accomplishments. Open House may include student performances, displays of work, or a combination of both.

Preparing for Back-to-School Night or Open House

As you're preparing for your first Back-to-School Night or Open House, follow these tips to make sure you're ready for the event:

- Decorate your room as cheerfully as possible.

- Plan some refreshments (often served in the cafeteria).

- Take photos of each individual student ahead of time and have double prints made (one for display and one to give to the parents).

- Display photos of class activities, including field trips, special science projects, and so on. (This helps your classroom appear to be academically stimulating and socially enjoyable.)

- Have your students clean and organize their desks. Parents invariably peek inside their children's desks and you don't want them to find anything upsetting, such as a dead snake or a moldy, two-week-old sandwich. Have your students place name tags on their desks.

- Display work for each and every student in your class, preferably the best paper they've written, the highest math score, or most attractive art project.

- If you teach primary grades, you may want to prepare black profiles (silhouettes) of each child. You can do these easily with an opaque projector that shines a strong light against the child's profile, projecting it directly onto black construction paper. Trace around the profile and then cut it out and put it on display. This can be a nice gift for each parent on the night of the Open House.

- Prepare and mail written invitations (as opposed to sending them home with the students). You may want the invitations to include a note, such as: "Due to time constraints, no private conferences, please."

- Prepare parent questionnaires that include the parent's name, address, telephone number, areas of expertise, and whether they are willing to share a skill, chaperone a dance or field trip, serve as room parent, help with fundraising, serve bus duty, help with tutoring, and so on.

- If you are preparing for a Back-to-School Night, work on your presentation (daily schedule, classroom rules, a sample lesson, a display of textbooks and materials, homework and absentee policies, dress codes, and behavior expectations). Some teachers like to take the parents through a typical school day, including mini-lessons and hands-on projects they can do while sitting at their children's desks. Your presentation will vary, of course, by grade level.

Goals for a Successful Back-to-School Night or Open House

Your primary mission on either of these nights is to gain the parents' trust. This means that they must take you seriously. For them to do so, you must take them seriously as well. You want them to believe, above all, that your goal is to teach their children as much as possible. This means that, although you may have your own concerns, including problems adjusting to the teaching profession in general and their children in particular, you must come across as confident and enthusiastic. Be concerned for their children's welfare—it will win them over.

To establish a working relationship with your students' parents, you must be a good listener, listening with your heart as well as your head.

These are some characteristics parents want to see in teachers:

- Professionalism

- Sincerity (look them in the eye when talking with them!)

- Accessibility
- Friendliness
- Optimism
- Enthusiasm
- Sensitivity

Speaking of sensitivity, watch for any financial hardships that may exist in your students' families. This knowledge will be helpful later in the school year when you come up with field trips or projects that may be too expensive for some of them. We know of one teacher who provides work for certain poorer students, such as helping in the classroom after school or picking up litter from the playground, and so on. She pays these students out of her own pocket. Your local parent-teacher organization may also be able to provide similar kinds of "scholarships" for some of these students.

To encourage the spirit of teamwork between you and the parents, explain the importance of communication. Ask them to contact you if they have any questions or become aware of a problem. Tell them you'd rather they talk to you before converting the problem into back-fence gossip. One teacher always adds a little humor at this point with this old cliché: "I'll make a deal with you: I won't believe half of what your child tells me goes on at home if you won't believe half of what he says goes on at school." This is usually followed by some light chuckles, but the parents get the idea. (Of course, in these days of increasing abuse and neglect, you should never tune out a child who may be expressing legitimate concerns.)

You also will want to encourage your parents to monitor homework assignments and provide a quiet place to study at home.

One problem at these Back-to-School Nights or Open Houses is the parent who tries to corner you for a miniconference about his or her child. These nights are not designed for conferences; however, there are always certain parents who feel

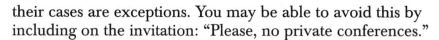

their cases are exceptions. You may be able to avoid this by including on the invitation: "Please, no private conferences."

For those parents who insist on approaching you for a private audience, cut it short, be polite, and move away into the crowd. If necessary, say something like, "She's doing fine so far; I'm looking forward to talking to you at conference time." If she's not doing fine or the parent is insistent, set up a conference with the parent in the near future.

Parent-Teacher Conferences

Your school policy will dictate the dates of parent-teacher conferences. Some schools have an initial conference at the end of the first quarter, followed by other conferences throughout the year only as necessary. Other schools set two per year, fall and spring. These conferences are provided in addition to report cards; however, when a conference is held at the end of a grading period, the teacher usually gives the report card to the parent at that time.

When setting specific conference times for parents who have more than one child in your school, it's smart to sit down with the staff and coordinate times so that the parents can see all their children's teachers consecutively.

Once you have scheduled tentative conferences with each parent, send home a form that says something like: "Here is your scheduled time. If you're unable to come at this time, when would be more convenient for you?" If you send this form a week to 10 days ahead of time, you'll be able to reschedule most of the conflicts. For those inevitable conflicts, try to reschedule within the upcoming week; sometimes a telephone conference works well if you have a problem getting together with the parents.

Remember that if you have any non-English-speaking parents and you don't speak their languages fluently, you will need a translator. Cluster these conferences together in blocks according to the availability of a translator.

Each conference usually lasts between 15 and 30 minutes; we think 20-minute segments are about right. Anything that needs to be said can usually be handled in this amount of time. It's important, by the way, that you stick to the schedule. Don't let one or two parents monopolize the time. It's inconsiderate to other parents who are waiting and complicates their meeting times with other teachers, as well. If a parent drones on and on and other parents are stacked up, politely remind the parent of the time factor. Apologize and say that you wish you had a little more time, but would it be convenient to schedule a continuation of the conference sometime next week? Usually the parent will get the idea, wrap it up, and leave without scheduling an additional conference.

Some teachers believe in setting a timer right on the desk or, worse yet, an alarm clock. Others use the ploy of glancing at their watches when the conference time is up. We feel that all of these tricks are rude and impersonal and should never be used.

Preparing for Parent-Teacher Conferences
Follow these tips to make sure you are ready to meet with your students' parents:

- Prepare notes for each conference, including the general strengths and weaknesses of each child. Look for the positive things to share with parents, followed by areas that need improvement. Point out as many strengths as possible during the conference. If the child has a few problems, try not to dump these on the parents unless the problems are serious, such as chronic lack of completed homework, repeated fighting, or use of unacceptable language. Just as you wouldn't send a student to the principal for chewing gum, don't burden parents with complaints that don't require their attention. Keep it to serious offenses, those things that will truly affect the child's ability to learn.

- Have the students' portfolios handy so that you can show parents their work, particularly in the areas of language arts and math. Try to have examples ready that show any improvement.

- In some cases, you might want to have the students' cumulative folders on hand to show a pattern of learning or behavior problems.

- Prepare the report cards, if they coincide with the dates of the conferences.

- Be sure that there is positive work for each student on display in the classroom; parents look for it. Also, be sure your classroom is neat and tidy.

- If you have a discipline system that includes listing names on the chalkboard, we recommend you erase these names during conference time. If a parent sees his child's name on the board as a disciplinary action, this won't create a positive, relaxed atmosphere for your conference. You can always write the names back on the board when conferences are over.

- Set up a comfortable waiting area for parents who arrive early, out of the weather and out of earshot of the conference in progress.

- Set up your conference area in the coziest setting possible; avoid having a desk between you and the parents. Try to sit face-to-face in the same size and type of chair. Don't use David Letterman's trick of sitting higher than his guests. This may intimidate the parent. Some teachers bring a bouquet of flowers, a dish of candy, a table lamp, potpourri, and toys for siblings to play with during the conferences. It's a bad idea to set up right next to a file cabinet—keep it homey! You're a team, remember?

Goals for Successful Parent-Teacher Conferences

The following list of do's and don'ts will help you make sure your first parent-teacher conferences go smoothly:

- The most important thing to remember is this: Listen 60 percent, talk 40 percent. These conferences aren't teacher filibusters; rather, they are designed for you to get the information you need from parents. You can't work as a team unless you know something about the student's family, interests, pets, and home.

- If you must discuss problem areas, emphasize the positive first, as mentioned earlier, and then gently mention the areas that need improvement. Remember, the child is the parents' most prized possession (or should be!), and some parents can easily be offended. Avoid comparing siblings unless you are comparing personality differences; don't compare academic abilities. Some parents are naive about this and will actually praise an older or younger sibling while criticizing your student during the conference itself, sometimes within earshot of your student. They might say something like, "Juan sure isn't doing as well as his sister did in fourth grade." If you hear a comment like this, try to be encouraging. Say something like, "Well, just wait a few years and you'll probably see it reverse itself."

- Make a concentrated effort to avoid using buzz words during the conference. Even though it's easy for them to come rolling out, expressions such as *whole language, holistic, cooperative learning,* or *behavior modification* will not only embarrass the parents (because they may not recognize the terms), but may make them think you're double-talking them or trying to impress them. There is no reason you can't conduct the entire conference using layman's language. If it's imperative to use a certain technical term, don't assume the parents know what it means. Explain the term simply and carefully. Communication is your goal, and buzz words hinder communication.

- Encourage parents to keep lines of communication open. Ask them to call you immediately if there is any question, problem, or inconsistency in what they are being told by the student at home.

- At times, you may want the student to sit in on the conference. Perhaps the student hasn't been honest with you— you may suspect that the child has lied about absences or forged a parental note. Having a face-to-face discussion with the parents in front of the student usually clears the air and brings this kind of dishonesty to a stop. Always end this type of parent-child conference with praise for the child in front of the parent. Not only does this balance out the negative part of the conference, but it's always good to praise children in front of others because many don't receive enough of it at home.

- Watch your body language. You want to appear open and sincere with parents, so be especially careful not to cross your arms. And remember, no clock-watching. Look them straight in the eyes when they are talking to you.

- If you have been having problems with a student, there may be a logical explanation that comes out during one of these conferences, such as a death in the family, serious illness, pending divorce, financial problems, Mom's left home, or Dad's in jail. If such information comes out during a conference, accept it with sensitivity and understanding. The important thing is to be a good listener.

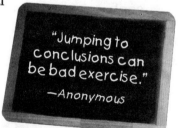
"Jumping to conclusions can be bad exercise."
—Anonymous

Try to end the conference on a positive note by pointing out something special about that particular child.

One important word of caution: Never assume that the person attending the conference is the student's mother, grandmother, sister, and so on. You can get yourself into hot water by making assumptions. Be prepared for the fact that the mother of a third-grader may look like the grandmother. Likewise, students have been known to sneak in an older sister to pass off as the mother, especially if the student suspects a bad report of some kind.

Following Up on Parent-Teacher Conferences

You thought you were finished, right? After the last parent-teacher conference is over, you still have some work to do, if you want to benefit from the large amount of information and your new contacts with parents. Here are a few tips for following up on parent-teacher conferences:

- You might find it helpful to send questionnaires to the parents after the conferences are over. These questionnaires should be optional and confidential. Ask questions such as "What did you like about the conferences? What did you dislike? Comments?" Be sure to emphasize the confidentiality of the parents' answers and stress your desire to work with them as a team. You'll find that by offering the parents a chance for feedback, they will be convinced of your sincerity.

- Remember that the walls in teachers' lounges may have big ears! Don't discuss your parent conferences in front of the staff. You'll be destroying the confidentiality of the conference, and this can get back to the parents in ways you won't expect.

Average gossip travels across town overnight—"juicy" gossip travels even faster.

Kindergarten Orientations

For those of you who are or will be teaching kindergarten, there are usually two orientations for the parents. The first is normally held during the year before the child starts school. This orientation is sometimes called a *Kindergarten Round-Up*. During this Round-Up, the parents are given an overview of what to expect when their children enter kindergarten. The school nurse usually attends this meeting to advise the parents on what is required to bring each child's health record up to compliance, including certain inoculations. The parents are also given some helpful ways to work with their children to prepare them for school.

The next orientation usually takes place right before the beginning of the school year. This meeting is not just for the children; it's especially for their nervous parents. You will probably never see parents with more anxiety than those sending off their first child to school.

Preparing for the Beginning-of-the-Year Orientation

Ask for a class list from your school secretary that includes the names, addresses, and telephone numbers of the parents of your new kindergartners. It's a good idea to send written invitations through the mail, followed by confirming telephone calls to any who haven't responded. Be sure to invite the children as well, including brothers and sisters.

Plan a short presentation that explains the daily schedule, as well as policies regarding the buses, lunch or breakfast, "Show-and-Tell," absences, safety habits, snacks, and the dates of Back-to-School Night and parent-teacher conferences.

Prepare sign-up lists for parent volunteers; you'll need plenty to help out as bus riders and in your classroom itself. Fortunately, more kindergarten parents volunteer than at any other grade level, so you'll probably have more than you need.

Be sure to round up enough adult-size chairs for this meeting. The smaller classroom chairs will not only be uncomfortable, but will hopefully be filled by the students and their siblings.

Prepare some refreshments; cookies and punch are fine.

Goals for a Successful Beginning-of-the-Year Orientation

Welcome the parents and siblings at the door with a pleasant smile. Remember that some parents may have a negative attitude toward school, often based on their own childhood fears or poor classroom experiences. Start off the meeting with the refreshments and then go into your presentation. Continually ask for questions; get them talking—it's your only way to uncover their fears and uncertainties.

Encourage the parents to teach their children to recite their addresses and telephone numbers before the first day of school if possible.

Hand out the volunteer sign-up sheets and hope for lots of signatures.

An important thing to remember is this: By the time children enter kindergarten, most of them are eager and excited—it's often the parents who need reassurance!

Report Cards

Because report-card time often coincides with conference time, parents may see report cards for the first time when you go over them at the conferences. One word of caution: Never let a problem fester until it shows up at the conference or on the report card. Protect yourself from parents' wrath by contacting them ahead of report-card time to give them a chance to help.

You will be expected to use the report card your district has chosen, along with its format. The use of letter grades usually starts about fourth grade; on report cards for kindergarten through third grade, normally only a child's progress is noted, such as "Needs Improvement," "Satisfactory," or "Excellent." Your main concern will be the space allotted for comments.

Here are some guidelines when making written comments on report cards:

- Be as truthful as possible without using strong or offensive language. After all, if there is a serious problem, you should have contacted the parent before report-card time.

- Be specific and avoid clichés. For example, instead of writing, "Can do better" or "Needs to improve effort," spell out the offense, such as "Turned in only 4 out of 15 homework assignments."

- Individualize and personalize the comments as much as possible.

- If you need to tell the parents more than you can fit into the comment section of the report card, call for a one-on-one conference with the parents.

- Be aware that many parents whose children usually receive *A*'s and *B*'s will question a *C* grade. Parents have different pain thresholds; some react only to an *F*, whereas others can be steaming over a *C*. By the way, most school districts have a rule that you can never give an *F* on the report card unless a formal progress report has gone home ahead of time warning the parents that their child is in danger of failing. This gives the parents time to work with their child and the teacher to bring up the grade.

Problem Parents

What? There are problem parents? You bet there are, and here are some of the most common types:

- **Parents addicted to drugs or alcohol.** You may very well encounter a problem with addictive parents. When these parents are under the influence, they may take it out on the teacher, either in a note, in a phone call, or during a conference. The best advice for handling this situation is to never stoop to their level. One teacher had to endure a nasty verbal attack by a drunk parent; however, the teacher remained calm and didn't argue because she knew that by lowering herself to the parent's level she would be fueling a fire that would eventually burn her. Use patience and tolerance with these parents.

If you have a sharp tongue, you may cut your own throat.

- **Parents with unrealistic expectations.**
  Some parents think their children are brilliant and

condemn them (and, perhaps, you) if they don't achieve at the parents' level of expectation. This is difficult for you as well as the child.

- **Abusive parents.** Unfortunately, in today's society we are encountering more and more abusive parents–those who mistreat their children physically or emotionally or neglect them. You should immediately report to your principal any signs of this type of abuse, as well as designated county social services officers.

- **Parents in denial.** You know the type: They will argue with you if you tactfully suggest that their children have stolen, lied, injured someone, forged a note, used unacceptable language, and so on. During a parent conference, you may suggest that their child has been cheating on exams or forging a signature, for example, but the parent's typical reply may be, "Well, he never did that at the other school. This is the first time I've heard of anything like this." What this parent doesn't realize is that the child's cumulative folder may contain comments from his past that show a history of this type of behavior. When you show parents the folder, they will still deny it. There really is no solution to these types of problem parents. One teacher said that he told a parent that her child was using certain vulgar words on the playground. The parent's reaction was "Well, what the hell's wrong with that?" You can see the futility!

> "The mother who fattens her child fattens a serpent."
> —Old Spanish proverb

Most parents are reasonable, mature, and cooperative; the problem parent is the exception and deserves your compassion. These difficult parents often have deep-seated problems stemming from their own childhoods.

Parent Volunteer Groups

You will run across two types of parent groups that have formal meetings. The first is called a *Parent Advisory Committee,* which is made up of parents, teachers, administrators, and possibly other staff members. The members of this committee are usually elected by their respective groups. The purpose of the committee is to furnish advice and recommendations to the school board regarding academic and special school programs. This committee is usually required by federal or state laws. The committee only advises, however; the school board makes the decisions.

The second type of group is usually known as the *PTO* (Parent-Teacher Organization), *PTA* (Parent-Teacher Association), or *PTS* (Parent-Teachers-Students). On the high-school level, the groups may be called something like *booster clubs.* Join your local organization and take advantage of all the good things they can do for you and your school.

Here are just a few of the things these groups can do:

- Raise funds to pay for things the district cannot afford, such as computers, art supplies, sports equipment, uniforms, special speakers, special field trips, playground equipment, and so on. They raise these funds in hundreds of ways, from selling Christmas wrapping paper, to cooking spaghetti dinners, to sponsoring community carnivals.

- Do thoughtful things for teachers throughout the year, such as honor them on their birthdays or retirements.

- Throw an appreciation banquet at the end of the year, honoring the teachers for their service.

- Provide volunteers from their group to help in the classroom, from career speakers, to teachers of skills and crafts, to room parents. Good room parents, by the way, are precious jewels! If you get one of these jewels, he or she will come to you to ask how he or she can help; they will plan special craft projects; and, best of all, they will plan your room parties, including all the food, decorations, games, and entertainment. You will notice that we said a "good" room parent is a jewel; a weak room parent (one who has to be told exactly what to do and how to do it) can be more of a liability than an asset.

Note: See www.pta.org, which includes more helpful ways parents and teachers can work together.

Conclusion

Remember this: The teacher can't give the child everything the child needs, and neither can the parent. But when they work together as a team, the child has the very best chance of succeeding!

Chapter 4

Preparing for Those Extracurriculars

As teachers, we are expected not only to teach, but also to participate in extracurricular activities. There are field trips to plan, funds to raise, guest speakers to invite, dances to chaperone, clubs to organize, and performances and sporting events to supervise. If these extracurriculars sound exhausting and time-consuming, you're right on both counts. They're part of any teacher's job description, however, and you need to be aware of what may be expected of you.

These activities, by the way, are not to be confused with those extras that are already part of each teacher's day, such as staff meetings, playground supervision, or lunch duties.

Field Trips

Field trips are especially common on the elementary grade level. They require planning and paperwork; parental permission; coordinating with the cooks, secretary, and bus driver; recruiting parent volunteers; and chaperoning and supervising the trip itself.

Planning the Field Trip

The first word of advice is that you should try to organize a field trip with the help of other staff members, particularly your principal and the teachers on your own grade level. You also need to be aware that there are certain trips traditionally taken each school year at each grade level; these may be discussed and scheduled at a staff or grade-level meeting. For example, the fourth-grade classes may always go to a certain museum or to the state capitol, and the primary-grade classes may traditionally get together before Halloween for a trip to a pumpkin patch.

Ask for your school's written policies regarding field trips. If there are no written policies, ask another teacher about policies and procedures. When you decide to organize a field trip on your own, be prepared to justify it to your principal, who may want to know how it coordinates with the subject matter you're teaching in your classroom. Once your field trip is scheduled and approved, you can go on to the next step: recruiting volunteers.

Recruiting Volunteers

Depending on the field trip and the age of your students, you will need approximately one adult for every seven or eight students (a lower student-per-adult ratio is even better, especially for primary grades). It's important to round up help as soon as your field trip schedule is set. If you asked the parents to fill out questionnaires at Back-to-School Night, you may already have a list of people willing to chaperone field trips. If you didn't send out questionnaires, try sending notes home with your students, asking for volunteers. If this doesn't work, ask your room parent to do some calling or talk to your local parent-teacher organization. By the way, it's always better to have more help than you think you'll need, especially if the excursion is the type of field trip where the children tend to spread out or where danger is involved.

Sending Permission Slips

You will need a legal permission slip from the parent of each student going on a field trip. Because students may lose these slips, forget to get them signed, and so on, it is a good idea to start this project early. Send out the first batch two weeks ahead of the planned trip; this gives you a chance to send home duplicates of the forms that get eaten by the family dog. Set your final deadline for receipt of these signed slips at least three days before the trip. There's nothing quite as frustrating as the student who comes running up to the bus on the day of the field trip, all raring to go—with no permission slip. He may have been home ill with the flu and long since crossed off the list of field trip participants, yet there he is, all smiles, expecting to hop on the bus. In a case like this, you might have your aide or the school secretary make an emergency call to the parents for their verbal permission. Of course, follow your school's policy in this type of last-minute crisis. If the policy requires that the child have written permission with no exceptions allowed, the child will have to stay behind.

If a parent is being asked to pay a fee for costs involved with the child's field trip, this request is usually included on the permission slip. If a parent is unable to pay, however, the child might not be excluded from the trip. Talk to your administrator regarding alternative funds for paying the child's fee.

Surprisingly, some parents won't give permission for their child to attend certain field trips. They may be overly protective, afraid that their child will get lost or the bus will be in an accident, and so on. You need to make special arrangements for these children to attend another class on the day of the trip. You will also need to furnish some work for them to do. Children may be sensitive about being placed in a lower grade level, so try to place them at their own grade level or the next grade up.

Notifying the School Staff

If you will be taking lunches on your trip, your cafeteria staff will need to have a lunch and milk count (an estimate will do) a couple of weeks before the trip. Then, three days or so before you leave, give them another updated count of sack lunches and milk needed.

On the morning of your departure, your secretary will want a class list indicating which students are going on the field trip and which are absent that day or staying behind in another classroom.

On the junior-high or high-school level, you may need to give the attendance officer this same information. (You should do this a week ahead of the field trip so that other teachers who have these students can plan for their absence.)

As you board the bus, the driver may ask for a list of kids, as well.

Find out from someone in the office what you should do with the permission slips. Sometimes you will be expected to take them along on the bus.

These are typical field-trip procedures, but, as always, check into the established policy for your particular school. When in doubt, find out from your principal, office personnel, or a veteran teacher.

Note: After the principal approves your trip, you should inform the district transportation service and coordinate the trip with them. As soon as possible, get a confirmation from your principal that everything is a "go" for your trip.

Supervising the Field Trip

Every field trip is an adventure. In fact, each trip has its own personality. After all our years of teaching, we still remember certain field trips because of unexpected things that happened or because of the personalities of those involved (including the volunteers).

Here is a collection of tried-and-true lessons we learned the hard way:

- **Lesson No. 1:** Do all student counts yourself! Never take anyone else's word for it—even that of your teaching aide or volunteer parent. If you're a new teacher, especially, you may not be aware of the cute little tricks some of the students may try. Some will scrunch down so that you can't see them; that's why we recommend a body count instead of a head count. Actually walk down the aisle and count *bodies*. If you don't, you could have 10 different head counts and 10 different totals—very time-consuming and frustrating. By the way, if the driver needs to make his own head count (or body count), fine, but you should still make your own to satisfy yourself that all students are accounted for.

- **Lesson No. 2:** Always take a box of small trash bags, paper towels, and moist Handi-Wipes on the bus! Why? Because Murphy's Law says that at least one of the kids will throw up, even though you will take precautions against it, such as cracking a couple windows (even in cold weather), forbidding any reading while the bus is moving, and having the queasy students sit up front. Murphy's Law also says that as soon as one child throws up, others will join in. In fact, the smell of vomit is known to travel from the front to the rear of a bus faster than the speed of light! If a real epidemic breaks out, have the driver pull over in a safe spot, preferably a rest area, and let the children walk around in the fresh air while the bus airs out. By the way, rarely will a child warn you that he is about to throw up, either because he is embarrassed, or the nausea may be a new experience for the child and he doesn't realize what comes next! Learn to look for the green faces and the expressionless eyes.

- **Lesson No. 3:** Don't make any assumptions! Don't assume that the adult chaperones will act like adults; don't assume that your well-behaved students will remain well-behaved; don't assume that your discipline problems will necessarily

If you can laugh at it, you can live with it!

misbehave; and don't assume that the trip will click along according to plan. In other words, try to have fun, enjoy the day, and stay flexible!

When it comes to the chaperones, you'll find that they have various pain thresholds when it comes to discipline. One parent literally let her little group of six run wild; in fact, they eventually took off, deciding to spend the afternoon shopping, tearing in and out of gift shops, buying ice cream, and so on. Meanwhile, we had no idea where they had gone. They never did go through the historical museum with the rest of the group, which was the purpose of the field trip in the first place. They eventually showed up at the bus, perfectly willing to share their field trip experience with the others. The parent said the kids wanted to go shopping instead and didn't think it mattered as long as they met back at the bus in time to return home. What logic!

Another parent had zero tolerance with the students. He was an off-duty security officer who volunteered to help chaperone the field trip; he was very strict and insisted that every student stand exactly where he told them to stand. We found out later that he actually handcuffed one unruly kid to the tour ship's handrail! Fortunately, the ship stayed afloat–try explaining to parents how it happened that their child went down with the ship!

When it comes to the children, some of the best-behaved can get out of hand on a field trip. Conversely, the one or two you anticipate creating havoc will surprise you by having a great, well-behaved day. We're reminded of a recent trip to a California mission. A fourth grader, who we were certain was going to be a problem for his chaperone, disappeared and we feared the worst. When found, he was on his knees at an altar, lighting a candle and praying for his grandmother! (This was for real–a chat with him later bore this out as we learned that she was, in fact, seriously ill.)

Other strange things can happen on field trips. One trip was timed to coincide with the annual return of the monarch butterflies to a certain spot in Pacific Grove, California. We studied this particular butterfly for two weeks before the trip and made a big deal out of it. But when we finally arrived at the spot—no butterflies! So, we improvised. We loaded the kids back into the bus, drove about a mile to an ocean beach, and ate our sack lunches while we ad-libbed a lesson in sea anemones. You need to be able to be creative when things don't go perfectly. After all, if you can just make it back home with no accidents, no sick kids, and a full body count, you will have had a successful field trip! (Note: A week later, while one of us was playing golf at a course near the butterfly grove, the monarchs were found hanging from the Monterey pines lining the second fairway. Apparently, the monarchs had not checked our field trip schedule!)

Fund-Raising

Because of tight financial times, school districts can't provide some of the things that used to be commonplace, such as certain classroom or playground equipment, books, supplies, special field trips, or even computers. That's why the teacher may become involved in fund-raising.

Let's begin by saying that your first choice should be to *delegate* this responsibility. If you have a sharp room parent, you may need only to put the bug in his or her ear and he or she may come up with a terrific idea. Or you may want to call on your local parent-teacher organization; tell them what you need and let them organize the fund-raising campaign.

If you're it as far as fund-raising is concerned, however, here are a few of the better ways to raise money:

- **Read-a-thon.** The idea of this fund-raiser is that your students will read books to raise money. You will need to design a sponsor form that the students will use to get sponsors to promise a certain amount of money per page, per book, or a flat dollar amount. After the students have read as much as they can by a given deadline, they go back and collect the money from their sponsors.

- **Collecting aluminum cans or other recyclable materials.** This idea is self-explanatory. You will, of course, need to provide bins and trash bags for the collection. (Warning: Don't be surprised if your classroom takes on the appearance of a city trash transfer site.)

- **Community service.** Organize a Community Service Day on which the students rake leaves, weed flower beds, wash cars, and so on to raise money. You need to be aware of insurance liabilities for these types of projects.

- **Bake sales.** Send home sign-up sheets for a bake sale to be held on the school premises or outside a cooperating local business.

- **Auctions.** Everyone loves an auction, and this can be a lot of fun. If you hold the sale as late in the year as possible, you will have time to gather items to be auctioned. You'll be amazed at the fascinating stuff that you can round up for one of these sales.

- **Carnivals.** A school or class carnival can be an excellent fund-raiser. Don't be surprised if you're asked to be dunked in a tank or hit in the face with a cream pie.

- **Halloween haunted house.** Turning your room or school cafeteria into a haunted house is another possibility. You know the routine: slimy noodles for "guts," cold grapes for "eyeballs," and so on.

- **Enchilada night, pizza night, spaghetti night.** Solicit help from local businesses to keep the costs down; double the cost per meal to determine the per-plate ticket price. By the way, those who may not otherwise be able to attend appreciate family tickets that give a price break.

All of these ideas are a lot of work, so learn the art of delegating. Depending on your grade level, your students and their parents may be able to do most of the work.

One key to the success of any fund-raiser is advertising. Start early and advertise in every way you can imagine, from local radio blurbs about community events, to flyers, to posters around school and in downtown businesses. Some small-town newspapers may provide a free news article about your project. One teacher even wore a sandwich board around town advertising his class's fund-raising event. (Now *that's* a dedicated teacher!)

Classroom Guests and Outside Speakers

Some of the extras you provide for your students may involve presentations from people in your community, or your students' family members who come in for a special day. Here are a few ideas for guest speakers and special events:

- **Career day speaker.** There are literally dozens of people living in your community who would be honored to speak to your class about their careers. Don't be afraid to ask busy professionals, such as a doctor, dentist, lawyer, or nurse; however, you should also seek out speakers with careers that don't require college degrees, such as carpenters, welders, or authors. Ask your speakers to bring tools of their trade; children love this added interest. Where do you find willing career speakers? From parent questionnaires prepared by your local parent-teacher organization or by asking people you know personally.

- **"Old-timer's" day.** Seniors are delighted to come to your classroom to tell your students their childhood tales, war stories, or other interesting experiences. Some of the locals have interesting stories specifically about your town, its history, and folklore.

- **Novelty speakers.** This type of speaker is usually a paid professional who entertains schoolchildren on a part-time or full-time basis. (His or her pay may come from one of the fund-raisers we spoke of earlier.) In our area, "49'er Bill" is one example of this type of speaker. He comes dressed for the part and puts on a complete program that includes a gold-panning exhibition. He plays the part to the hilt as he tells true stories of the Old West.

- **Speakers with a mission.** These speakers are easy to enlist because they are trained to make presentations to schoolchildren. D.A.R.E (Drug and Alcohol Resistance Education) supplies speakers who love to come as often as invited. The local fire department will also supply special speakers, as will the police. Smokey the Bear and McGruff are popular around campuses.

- **Grandparents' day.** This is a special day, usually organized by your local parent-teacher organization. If your school doesn't already have an annual grandparents' day, don't be afraid to plan one for your own class. The idea of this day is to honor the grandparents by providing a sit-down lunch with decorations (made by the students) and a special program performed by the students, as well. This is a great opportunity to have several of the willing grandparents tell about their childhoods, what they did for fun as a child, and how things have changed through the years. An interview format sometimes works well to get them talking. Ask your room parent to find a few parents who will help prepare and serve the luncheon.

In the case of any special speaker, ask a local television station and newspaper to cover the event. Also, take plenty of photos and videotape the presentation so that you can use it again in years to come.

After the presentation, have your students send thank-you notes, along with artwork showing what they liked best about the program.

School Dances

Most teachers would rather have root-canal work than chaperone a school dance, especially if it cuts into their family time on the weekend. On the other hand, these dances sometimes can be a lot of fun. Remember that the school dance is an important and positive addition to a student's educational experience. (Just think back to your own high school prom!)

As a chaperone, here are some of your responsibilities:

- Ask for direction from your school's administration. What is the policy on inappropriate music, guest passes, leaving and re-entering the dance, signing in and out of the dance, and so on?

- During the dance itself, watch for any signs of drug or alcohol use. Know your school's policy on handling these situations. Also, watch for any strange behavior, such as students getting sick (a sign of this use).

- Watch for any outsiders trying to crash the dance.

- Listen to the words of the music; be aware of any obscene lyrics.

- Be aware of any signs of gang activity (your administration will tell you what to look for).

One of the biggest teacher complaints is the volume of the music; we recommend wearing earplugs (seriously!). Some teachers beg for duty by the back gate, which is usually quieter and a little more trouble-free.

Instead of live music, you'll probably have a disc jockey. One problem with DJs is that they may play whatever the kids request, which is where you'll need to monitor lyrics carefully.

Most schools have rules that require guest passes for dates invited from other schools. A deadline is usually issued for requesting these passes; for a Friday-night dance, for example, the deadline may be 3:30 p.m. the previous Wednesday. The deadline is set a couple of days ahead of the dance so that the guest can be checked out (usually by calling the administration at the guest's school).

At one high school, this deadline was adhered to without exception until a special situation came up involving a nerdish fellow who had never had a date for one of these dances. He came into the office late Friday afternoon desperately needing a guest pass for a girl he invited to the sophomore dance that night. He was told, "You know, you needed to make this request no later than Wednesday." The boy replied, "But this is a special situation—I just met her today!"

The administrator involved bent the law a bit and issued a guest pass, realizing that sometimes it doesn't hurt to be a little flexible. He knew the boy could have been devastated socially and emotionally if he had denied the pass. The moral of the story is this: Be a sensitive listener and know when to cut a little slack, no matter what the situation is. (By the way, the last time we heard from the boy, he and his date were seniors in high school and still dating!)

"There is no rule without an exception."
—Cervantes

Don't be surprised if you find yourself dancing at one of these occasions! It has become popular for schools to sponsor "Bridging the Gap" dances, during which the students teach parents and teachers their dances and then the adults teach the students some from their era. Such a dance requires a sharp DJ who has a supply of several styles of music.

At one of these Bridging the Gap dances, a girl asked an older male teacher to dance. He said he wasn't comfortable with any of the new dances. So she cheerfully suggested, "How about the 'Mashed Potato' instead?" He smiled and said, "Actually, I was thinking more of the Charleston!"

Team Sports Events

You may also be required to spend some weekends supervising a team sports event, such as a football or basketball game. Just as a school dance contributes to a student's total educational experience, these games are also an important part of a student's school years.

Here are some of the problems you will need to watch for during these games:

- **Fighting.** Prevent fights by keeping opposing fans on their own side of the gym or stadium. You'll find that fights usually break out when a few students from one school wander across to the "other side." You can prevent your own students from doing this by addressing it ahead of time, preferably at the pep rally or during an assembly. The problem is how to keep the opposing students from filtering over to the stands on your side of the field or gym. Your administration should be in contact with the opponent's administration to seek cooperation in this matter.

- **Unsupervised children.** You may be expected to supervise younger children dropped off by parents. It may shock you to know that many parents drop their younger children at high school games while they go out to dinner, go shopping, and so on. They deliberately use you as a baby-sitter, and this can become a real hassle. The kids think they have free reign to run around, annoy the spectators, horse around with other kids, and generally use the gym or field as their playground. The situation really gets touchy if the parents are present and they are allowing their children to tear around and cause problems. There is a fine line between supervising these children and offending their parents.

- **Substance abuse or gangs.** Watch for signs of drug or alcohol abuse and gang activity. Work with the security officers on duty and follow the policies your school's administration has established for handling these incidents. Unfortunately, in this day and age there is such potential for these problems that many districts have eliminated all night games, scheduled games at a neutral site, and set strict rules, such as not allowing students to return to an event once they have left the premises.

You never know what you'll have to deal with at these sports events; however, you'll never be bored, that's for sure. One of the funniest stories we ever heard was a situation that happened at a basketball game. A male teacher was on duty when a girl ran up to him in a panic. He asked what was wrong. She said, "Come quick—she can't get out!" He said, "What do you mean 'she can't get out'? Who?" The girl replied, "Come see!"

He followed her to the top row of the bleachers; she pointed down between the bleachers and the back wall of the gym. There hung a girl, suspended by her well-endowed upper torso. Evidently, she had dropped something behind the bleachers, tried to climb down to get it, and got hung up instead. He knew the solution, but in today's "sexual harassment environment" he was afraid to suggest it. He went to find a woman teacher, who suggested that the girl unhook her bra. This changed her contour just enough to pop her loose. The girl wasn't a bit embarrassed by the incident; the same cannot be said for the male teacher.

Clubs and Organizations

You also may be asked to sponsor a club or organization, such as the Spanish, Drama, or Debate Club. Your department may expect this type of duty, and it often includes a stipend.

Conclusion

All of these extracurricular activities come with the territory. The sooner you learn to accept them as part of your profession, the better. Some teachers view these activities as duties; others accept them as part of their job. The former dread the activities and spend long evenings policing the events. The latter go with the flow, interacting with the students in the non-classroom setting, and have a reasonably enjoyable evening.

Chapter 5

The Teacher's Many Hats

I t won't take you long to realize that a teacher must be many things—a surrogate parent, friend, social worker, provider, psychologist, nurse, emergency worker, and counselor. No wonder this is such a hard job! All this started many years ago when the teacher taught in a one-room school-house. Not only did she teach all the grades, but she started the fire in the wood stove in the morning and cleaned the school-house at the end of the day. Today, we merely flip the switch on the thermostat and leave the cleaning to the custodians, but our society's complexities have actually given us more respon-sibilities than teachers ever had in years past.

> **Encouraging Words from Our Survey**
>
> "Welcome and good luck! Remember, we all have a first year."
>
> —A high-school teacher with 12 years of experience.

These responsibilities can seem overwhelming, espe-cially to new teachers, which is why we have sprinkled "Encouraging Words from Our Survey" throughout this chapter. We want you to think of the many hats you wear as opportunities, not burdens.

Surrogate Parent

During the hours when a student is in your class, you are that student's "surrogate parent"; in fact, educational codes even go so far as to spell out the fact that legally you are *en loco parentis*, the acting parent of that child. You actually become an extension of your students' homes, which means that you are expected to care for them, their welfare, and their safety. You are to nurture them, build their self-esteem, discipline fairly, and be aware of their needs. The educational codes also give you the authority to teach values and morals, including manners and social skills.

Children don't stop being children when they arrive on the school grounds. Many still suck their thumbs, wet their pants, and need their mommies. This is especially true for kindergartners, but you'll see the "umbilical problem" in older students as well. You need to be sensitive to your students' needs, which may mean stepping in and protecting a child if he feels threatened by a bully who may be hanging around after school to "get him." Are you responsible to see that your student gets home safely? Yes, you are.

A good example of this is a fourth-grade boy who was threatened by a ninth-grade boy because the fourth-grader had been teasing the older boy's younger sister. We noticed this older boy hanging around the school grounds when school let out, so we notified the principal, the other staff members, and the fourth-grader's parents. Then we walked the child to his home every day until the problem was settled.

> **Encouraging Words from Our Survey**
>
> "Hang on for three years—don't give up."
>
> —A primary teacher with four years of experience.

As you take on the role of surrogate parent, this is a good rule of thumb: Do what would come naturally if you were the child's own parent. One of the very sad things you'll find as you enter the teaching profession is that occasionally you will care more than the child's own parents.

Friend

One of your most important roles as a teacher is to be a friend to your students. You may be the only positive role model in a child's life and, sadly, you may be the only adult who actually likes him. The child's only other role model may be a father who is in prison, the leader of big brother's gang, or a violent character on a TV show.

The question, however, is this: How can you be a "friend," "buddy," or "pal" without losing your authority as "teacher"? It's OK to toss a football with a student, shoot hoops, or play a game of chess. You also can show you care through praise, appropriate joking and teasing, and by being a good listener. Also, a simple question such as "How's it going?" can show that you're interested in the child's life. What you want to avoid is "getting down and becoming one of them" through inappropriate behavior, such as physically wrestling with them on the ground or "bouncing" a child on your knee.

Through all our years of teaching, we have seen many students change from rebels and discipline problems to children who want to please and behave, just because of trust and friendship that grew during the school year. A good example is a fifth-grade boy who was one of the most rebellious kids who ever came through the school—he really made life miserable for the staff. Finally, one teacher decided to befriend this kid by building up his self-esteem, laughing and joking with him, and showing that he actually liked the boy.

The teacher noticed that the boy was a very good dancer, so he got a cassette tape and had the boy teach eight other students how to dance to the music. The boy thrived on this attention and the chance to shine in front of his peers. After a few days of practice, the student and his "dance troupe" performed for several teachers and their classes and the boy slowly began to trust his teacher and like school in general. By the end of the school year, this tough kid had mellowed to the point where he didn't want to leave after the last day of classes.

He hung around the classroom, asking if he could help, and then confessed, with tears in his eyes, "I don't want school to be over—I don't want to go to middle school next year."

There are many success stories like this one, including another problem kid whose high-school football coach befriended him during his senior year. The coach recognized the boy's athletic talents and talked them up to the boy's peers. The boy made a turnaround, went on to college, and became a second-round pick in the NFL draft.

Is it any wonder that when children are asked what they want to be when they grow up, many say, "a teacher"?

> **Encouraging Words from Our Survey**
>
> "Laugh! At yourself and situations, because you *will* survive!"
>
> —An elementary principal with 29 years of experience.

Social Worker

As social worker, you wear a very important hat because you become the liaison between the school, the home, and social agencies. You are responsible to watch out for the health and welfare of all your students. Be aware; be alert; watch for red flags! Don't become so engrossed in your teaching responsibilities that you let those red flags wave unnoticed. You may be the first person to notice a child's needs; the school nurse cares as much as you do, but she doesn't live in your classroom day in and day out. Nor does the psychologist or social worker.

Use your eyes and ears throughout the day. It's OK to eavesdrop on conversations now and then. One child may mention to another that nobody's home at night or that an "uncle" is mean. Another red flag is a child who doesn't seem to be eating lunch. Ask the child why. Often, he or she will say "I'm not hungry." But the real reason might be that the parent didn't pack a lunch or didn't provide lunch money. In a case like this, you may want to call home to find out why. If the parents don't have money to buy food or school lunches, don't be afraid to take charge of the situation; initiate the application form through proper channels for free or reduced lunches for the child.

Another red flag may be the girl who arrives on a windy, wintry day wearing a thin cotton dress and a flimsy sweater. Why is she the only child without a warm jacket and hat? Ask her—get to the bottom of it.

Notice your students' physical appearances as well. Is hair uncombed? Do some wear dirty clothes? Are there dental problems? There is often a history of neglect or abuse that runs in families; ask your school nurse or secretary about any older siblings who had similar problems.

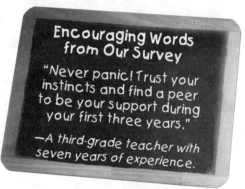

Encouraging Words from Our Survey

"Never panic! Trust your instincts and find a peer to be your support during your first three years."

—A third-grade teacher with seven years of experience.

The "social worker" hat is heavy with responsibility, it's true. But it's one of your most important roles as teacher.

Provider

Teachers are notoriously compassionate, sacrificial people, so it's no wonder our hearts break when we see poor children who need clothing and school supplies. Their parents may be doing the best they can, but with many children in the family and a low income, it may not be possible to provide as they would like.

Here is where you take on the role of "provider." You can either provide for the child out of your own pocket, as many teachers do, or you can find another way. If you want to handle the problem yourself, you can gather up jackets, shoes, and other clothing from friends or family members whose children have outgrown them. As another alternative, you can purchase children's clothing at garage sales.

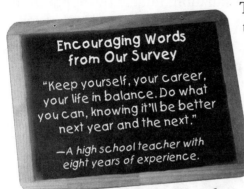

Encouraging Words from Our Survey

"Keep yourself, your career, your life in balance. Do what you can, knowing it'll be better next year and the next."

—A high school teacher with eight years of experience.

There are several other ways to provide clothing to the poor, including a clothing drive sponsored by your school. Talk to your administrator about the possibility of interested parents acquiring clothing for needy students. These items can be kept in a designated room for future needs. More and more schools are providing a room like this, along with an ongoing clothing drive throughout the school year.

Most PTA groups are more than willing to provide clothing for needy students; the same can be said for local service organizations. Give them a precise list of what your students need, including the age, sex, and sizes of each child. The same goes for school supplies; tell them exactly what a certain student needs.

Psychologist

In your psychologist role, you need to be a good listener, advisor, problem solver, comforter, family counselor, and, most importantly, observer. Because you are with your students all day, you'll become aware of their emotional and psychological needs. Watch for depression, temper flares, frequent crying, hyperactivity, sleepiness, and mood swings (up one day, down the next). Has a student recently lost a family member? How is he or she handling the grief? Does a child get "hurt" too easily? Be alert for potential problems.

It's surprising how many problems come to light during a parent-teacher conference. You may hear for the first time that a family member has died or is in jail, or that the child's parents are getting a divorce, which is one of the most common and devastating problems of all.

Be aware that some of the students with more serious problems go unnoticed because they aren't causing trouble for the teacher. For example, it may not occur to you that certain well-behaved children may actually be isolates (see chapter 2). These children are neither high achievers nor discipline problems, but they fall into a middle group that teachers usually don't notice. These isolates are often shy loners who need positive recognition every day, but don't get it because their insecurities are "invisible." Their numbers are not great, but almost every class has one or more of these students. We sometimes wonder how many antisocial acts in later years might have been avoided had someone noticed an isolate's plight and taken a personal interest.

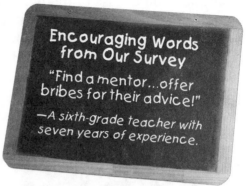

Encouraging Words from Our Survey

"Find a mentor...offer bribes for their advice!"

—A sixth-grade teacher with seven years of experience.

Other students may blend in with the woodwork because they are quiet and "good," and yet they may be suffering from depression or be under the influence of drugs or alcohol. And don't think drugs and alcohol are found only in the upper grades; they are becoming more prevalent in lower grades as well. Sadly, an example of this is a situation that involved a kindergarten student in Colorado. The teacher noticed that the child was often sleepy and lethargic; it turns out that the child smoked marijuana on a regular basis. The parents were dealers who encouraged their own children to smoke the drug. The county child abuse and neglect agency got involved, resulting in a police raid and arrests.

If you sense that any of your students needs help, don't be afraid to ask for it. If you're not exactly sure who to go to for referral, start with your mentor teacher or principal. Because you care enough to watch out for your students' needs, you may save a child from a lifetime of failure or destruction. For example, a mild dose of medication may calm a hyperactive student, enabling him to concentrate, learn, and enjoy school. Or, you may discover a student has an alcoholic parent; a simple referral may result in family counseling that not only helps your student, but saves the parents' marriage and brings peace to the siblings as well.

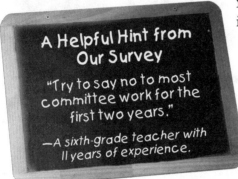

A Helpful Hint from
Our Survey

"Try to say no to most committee work for the first two years."

—A sixth-grade teacher with 11 years of experience.

You can easily get caught up in the teaching day, so make a point to sit down once in a while to focus on each child's psychological well-being. Most school districts and local governments provide professionals who are trained to help, but you need to recognize the needs and make the referrals.

Nurse

Your school nurse is counting on you to refer students who have general health problems such as open sores, ringworm, communicable diseases, lice, menstrual pain, fevers, and so on. You should also refer students with hygiene problems, including body odor.

In the case of emergencies, however, you need to know first-aid procedures. Your district has probably required you to take CPR and first-aid classes; if not, take them on your own because you'll need them! Many districts also require their teachers to attend in-services on the subject of blood-borne pathogens, such as Hepatitis B Virus (HBV) and Human Immunodeficiency Virus (HIV). One of the most important things you'll learn in this class is the danger of exposing yourself to blood and other body fluids. You may find a student bleeding after a playground fall or fight. You are required to wear rubber gloves anytime you're handling or treating a child who is bleeding, whether caused by an accident or due to a health problem. Not only should you be careful whenever blood is involved, but you should keep the rest of the students away from it as well.

Be aware of your school's emergency procedures in case of a serious accident. If you need an ambulance or the assistance of a nurse or administrator, send another student for help while you stay with the injured child. Give appropriate first aid until help arrives, observing required precautions if there is bleeding.

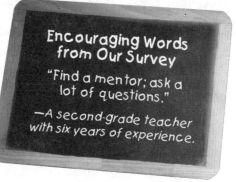

Encouraging Words from Our Survey

"Find a mentor; ask a lot of questions."

—A second-grade teacher with six years of experience.

We could write another entire book on the "nurse hat" we've worn during our years of teaching. There have been horrifying incidents, such as the time a child was run over by a bus in front of school. Both back wheels ran over the student, but, miraculously, he was not seriously injured. In another case, a kindergarten girl was crying because her nose hurt. Eventually a doctor found an antennae—a little green piece of plastic—from a game called Cootie. The antennae had been crammed all the way up her nose—no wonder she was in pain!

In another case, a boy fell off his bike, which resulted in an exam by a doctor, who discovered a piece of eraser imbedded inside his ear. The eraser turned out to be a bullet shot from an eraser gun about two years before. No wonder the kid was having trouble hearing. Once the doctor

Encouraging Words from Our Survey

"Be yourself. Don't try to do too much extra. Pace yourself and don't be intimidated by creative, high-energy, veteran teachers."

—Anonymous

removed the bullet, the student could hear so well he kept saying "Don't shout!"

Emergency Worker

When you don this hat, you should be ready to handle any emergency: fire, bomb threat, earthquake, tornado, flood, hurricane, or kidnapping attempt.

Your district will instruct you in the emergency procedures they expect you to follow in any of these situations, and you'll need to conduct classroom drills so that your students will know exactly what to do in every case. Let's hope you never experience any of these emergencies, but you still need to train your students well.

The biggest danger to your students may be a kidnapping or abduction attempt. You'll need to spend time talking to your class about this risk. Don't let one of your students end up on a milk carton!

Here are some precautions you can take to prevent an abduction from happening:

- Warn your students, as frankly as possible, about the people out there looking to prey on children. (Many parents have never spoken candidly with their children.)

 Caution: The goal of these warnings is to increase awareness, not give the children nightmares!

- Watch for suspicious characters hanging around the school campus, or driving or walking by. Take a pad of paper and a pencil with you on yard duty so that you can copy the license numbers of cars that seem to be cruising by regularly. Report anyone lurking around the school; then let the authorities handle any investigation. By the way, there are strict laws that prohibit loitering around school properties.

- Be careful of who picks up a child from school. Be aware of court orders giving one parent or the other custody of a child. Important: Don't take a parent's word for such a court order; ask to see it with your own eyes. Also, don't necessarily believe what the child tells you; he or she may have a preference for one parent over the other. Office personnel usually will advise you of these situations. If you discover the problem on your own, be sure to advise your administrator and school secretary.

> **Encouraging Words from Our Survey**
>
> "Give education a chance. The process of teaching gets easier the longer you are immersed."
>
> —A sixth-grade teacher with three years of experience.

 Note: See "Support Groups" in the appendix for helpful Web sites and teacher-support newsgroups.

Conclusion

Yes, as teachers we are required to wear many different hats. The important thing is not to let this go to our heads (no pun intended!).

We need to remember that Psych 101 doesn't make us psychologists and Red Cross first-aid certificates don't make us paramedics. We are qualified teachers, however, which gives us the authority and responsibility to refer children to professionals in other fields who wear the real hats. Meanwhile, in spite of our duties to nurture, praise, and love our students, what our country needs more than ever are good academic teachers—and we are fortunate because we get to wear that most important hat of all!

Part II

Preparing Your Classroom

Chapter 6

The Classroom Environment

Your classroom environment is one of the few things within your control and it should reflect your unique personality. This is especially true if you have a self-contained classroom that becomes your "home away from home" every school day. The classroom is also home to your students, so you want it to be a happy, comfortable setting with a friendly feeling, conducive to their learning and emotional well-being. You also want to create an environment that gives your students a feeling of family, where they feel welcomed and loved regardless of their social or cultural backgrounds.

The General Room Environment

The way desks are arranged, the traffic flow, the lighting, and more subtle effects such as noise level, temperature, and air quality all contribute to your classroom's overall environment. The following sections give you ideas on how to use these aspects to make your space more homey.

Traffic Flow

Before the school year begins, you will need to decide on the overall arrangement of your room—where do you want your desk? How should you arrange the students' desks? How many interest centers do you want, and where should you place them? As you sketch out your ideas, be careful not to fill up every square foot of the room—leave traffic paths, not only for you to maneuver, but also for the children themselves.

Be sure to leave an open area inside the main door of your classroom; this is where the most bodies will be at any one time. Your students will tend to bunch up in this open space as they arrive and, of course, you need plenty of room whenever they line up at the door. Having an entry area free of barriers and obstructions is important—this gives students an open invitation to this "home."

You will also need some space around your desk, the pencil sharpener, the water fountain, and the sink.

Desk Arrangements

During our years of teaching we have used various classroom setups, and there is no right or wrong way to arrange desks. Depending on the number of students, their needs, and your teaching style, you may choose a plan that makes sense to you.

Here are five popular classroom arrangements:

- **Traditional.** In the traditional classroom setup, you have six rows of five with the desks lined up one behind the other, like soldiers.

- **Three clusters.** In this arrangement, you have three separate clusters of desks, each with approximately 10 desks.

- **Four clusters.** Each cluster has seven or eight desks; the clusters are angled so that all the students face the center—a kind of "theater-in-the-round."

- **Semicircle.** Arrange desks into two semicircles that face your desk. Be sure to stagger the desks so that each student has full view of you and the chalkboard.

- **Cooperative learning clusters.** Each cluster is a block of desks fit tightly together to facilitate the learning activities that typically go on in a cooperative group setting.

These five choices are based on the assumption that your classroom is furnished with individual desks. Some classrooms have tables, which, of course, provide you with instant clusters, although there is some flexibility in their arrangement. If your room has desks, but you prefer tables, don't be afraid to mention this to your administrator. There may be a storage room full of extra classroom furniture, or another teacher may have tables and prefer desks. A simple switch will make you both happy.

Whatever you decide, be sure to check the following items:

- You can see all the students from the front of the room.

- You have enough space to walk.

- The students can see you, as well as the chalkboard, maps, and so on.

- You can move freely among the individual students.

If you're the newest teacher on staff, you may wonder why your room is such a hodgepodge of furniture! Your desk chair may be wobbly, the filing cabinet tipsy, and nothing seems to match. The reason may be that in some schools, when a teacher leaves, the other teachers cannibalize the room. You'll notice that the teachers who have been on staff the longest seem to have the most attractive classroom furniture. That's because they've been trading desks, filing cabinets, and tables for years. So don't be surprised if you have to put up with the leftovers for a while.

One thing you can do, however, is be sure each desk is the proper size for each student and adjusted for that student's comfort. You would never expect an adult office worker to sit at an uncomfortable desk for even one day, much less a whole year. Yet many teachers expect their students to make do with desks that are too big, small, high, low, or wobbly. If you have a tiny student in your upper-grade classroom, ask to borrow a smaller desk or table from a primary classroom. Likewise, if you're teaching first grade and have an oversized student, borrow a larger desk.

Once you have a desk to fit each child, have the custodian adjust for height and correct any wobbles. Better yet, buy your own Allen wrench, which seems to be the necessary tool for most desk types, so you can easily make adjustments yourself without having to call the custodian. Be aware that you may need to adjust these desks during the year; some kids grow at amazing rates.

Sound Control

The classroom's noise level reflects the teacher's personality, falling somewhere between a morgue and a discotheque. The important thing is for the children to feel comfortable in your classroom. They may not perform well in a setting that is either too chaotic or too boring.

Some teachers play music softly in the background during some activities, which can provide a calm learning environment. However, students generally perform better in a quieter setting.

If you tend to kill off your live plants, replace them with silk ones.

Plants

Live plants are a nice touch in a classroom and give a homey feeling. We've never had much luck keeping the blasted things alive, but they're still a good idea!

Incandescent Lighting

Classrooms usually have ceilings of fluorescent lights; this type of lighting, although efficient, is cold and impersonal. You may want to scatter a few lamps around your classroom, the type that use regular incandescent lightbulbs. Place them on counters or at several of the interest centers. The glow of incandescent lighting will give a warm ambience to your classroom.

Room Temperature

Whether the weather outside is cold or hot, it's important that you keep your classroom at a comfortable temperature, usually toward the cool side. If you don't monitor this carefully, you may notice your students starting to yawn. If this happens, have them stand and stretch; or you may want to have the class shift gears and do something lively for a while, such as sing.

Smells

A professor at Yale University did a study that proved that a student's sense of smell is the most powerful of all the senses. He says that a classroom should be filled with smells of home, such as fruit, flowers, or foods. The best way to accomplish this in the classroom is by simmering potpourri that has these homey scents. Many teachers keep a potpourri pot going all day.

Walls and Bulletin Boards

You don't need us to tell you how to decorate your walls and bulletin boards; there certainly are enough books available that can give you hundreds of ideas and specific instructions. However, we do want to pass on a few general things we have learned  through the years that can help enhance the environment you create.

Easy frames for bulletin boards: string or yarn.

First of all, you need to be careful when selecting the colors you use on your walls. A popular in-service for teachers features a "classroom environmental specialist" who preaches the importance of color selections. She especially dislikes the use of orange and yellow in a classroom because they tend to excite the students by raising their blood pressures. However, blues, greens, and pastels are calming, and pale pink or peach is especially soothing, which is why these colors are used on prison walls. We had one of these experts deliver an in-service at our school, and by the end of the school year, except for a brief time before Halloween, the rack of orange butcher paper in our teacher supply room was barely touched!

For added color, cover a few bulletin boards with inexpensive print fabric.

If you're in an older school, you may have fixed framed bulletin boards and old-fashioned chalkboards. The newer schools usually have entire walls covered with tack board, with no defined spaces. You can create your own frames by using borders, which give you greater control of your classroom decor.

Here are some general guidelines you can follow when decorating your walls and bulletin boards:

- **Top third of the walls:** If you decorate this space at all, use it for large lettering, murals, borders, and large pictures (animals, clouds, trees, and so on).

- **Lower two-thirds of the walls:** Use this space to display anything that has small detail, such as the students' writing or math work, or smaller pictures. You want your students to be able to see this type of display at their own eye level. If you're a primary teacher, place the work even lower on the wall. Many teachers forget about their "little people" and place detailed work at their own eye level.

- **Strive for colorful and eye-catching wall displays without cluttering your walls.** Some teachers think they are expected to fill every square inch of wall space; they don't realize that this can actually create a claustrophobic and confusing environment. The moral? Leave a little space around your displays.

Here are some display ideas that we have used through the years:

- **Seasonal.** A seasonal display could be called "Signs of Fall" (an arrangement of leaves, pictures, and so on) or "Signs of Winter" (snowflakes or snow scenes).

- **Student work.** This space is reserved for the students' current work (stories, writing samples, and so on). One teacher has a giant gray whale that he puts on the same wall every school year. Under the whale he has the title "Whale of a Job." He uses this space to feature various examples of his students' outstanding work. (He gets teased by the other staff members about the giant whale, but it works for him.) A bulletin board like this can be a time-saving idea. It's important to vary the students' work.

Wear a carpenter's apron and a wrist pincushion as you decorate your room. It keeps everything handy and saves time.

- **Holidays and calendar.** This space includes the monthly calendar along with a display featuring a holiday within the month.

- **Birthday board.** This board has a chart with the date of each student's birthday, including the specific birthdays in that month.

- **Student recognition board.** This is the space for your Student of the Week or Student of the Month awards, along with photos of these award-winning students. You can also use this space to display photos of your students participating in various activities (field trips, the Christmas play, singing, athletics, and so on).

- **Artwork.** You may want a separate space to display current artwork that's included in your overall theme.

- **Social science.** Here is the place for maps and displays pertaining to your current social-science project.

Interest Centers

Interest centers, also known as *learning centers,* are tables or counters located around the perimeter of a classroom. Each center has its own purpose and affords students different modes of learning. As you recall from your teacher training, there are three basic types of learners: visual, auditory, and kinesthetic. The visual learner may prefer the AV center, where he can see something for himself on a television screen. The auditory learner will enjoy hearing as she listens to cassette tapes, and the kinesthetic learner will probably lean toward the manipulatives available at various interest centers.

These centers serve as valuable teaching aids by allowing students the freedom to choose learning arenas they prefer. If you have 30 children in your classroom, you won't always know which students favor a particular mode of learning. By furnishing these learning centers, you give the students the chance to learn by doing, hearing, or seeing.

The use of these centers can be a special privilege that you give as a student reward. These learning centers offer valuable side benefits; they teach a child to work alone and to concentrate while other class activities are going on. This may help the student study independently in the years to come.

The following sections explore a few centers we have seen work well.

The Reading Center

Make this center as inviting and cozy as possible by providing a good reading lamp, carpet pieces, pillows, beanbag chairs, or overstuffed furniture; this will encourage the students to relax and get comfortable while reading. You may be able to furnish your reading center very inexpensively by picking up a few things at garage sales.

This center should offer a variety of books and resource materials including the following:

- **Recreational paperbacks.** Try to find a display rack (like the type you see in the grocery stores) that holds a large number of books in a small space. Fill this rack with donated paperbacks and extra books you may order from a book club (such as Scholastic Book Club, Arrow Book

Club, Troll Books, or Discovery Books). Also, watch for children's books at garage sales and flea markets. Your own school's resource center may be able to furnish books for your library as well. Send home a note to the parents, too, asking for any books they may want to donate. Public libraries also have giveaways from time to time. Finally, you may want to consider a contest where you offer the class some type of party (ice cream, pizza, and so on) depending on the number of books they can gather. If you have a bilingual classroom, it's a good idea to have books in English, Spanish, and other languages spoken in your classroom.

We have found that it's a good idea to restrict the use of these books to the classroom because it's too easy for them to become lost. You may want to use a checkout system. Don't be surprised, by the way, when books begin to disappear within the classroom. You always have one or two pack rats who squirrel away a book inside their desks. It's a good idea to have all your students empty and clean out their desks regularly throughout the year—you'll be surprised what turns up!

- **Hardback books.** School-owned classic hardbacks may be furnished to you in sets. Be especially careful to keep track of these because you'll need to account for them at the end of the school year.

- **Magazines.** There are many excellent magazines of interest to elementary-age children, including the following:

  - *Cobblestone*
  - *Stone Soup*
  - *National Geographic World*
  - *Boy's Life*
  - *Chickadee*

    ⌀ Ranger Rick

    ⌀ Odyssey

Much of the material in these magazines is not dated and is always interesting. You can easily get past issues of these publications from parents whose children have outgrown them.

The Reference Center

If space is limited, you may want to combine the reference center with the reading center. Here are a few of the things usually found in the reference center:

- **Globe.**

- **Maps.** Display maps showing the countries of origin for any of your bilingual students, maps of your own community, and even aerial photos of your community (available through your Chamber of Commerce, the local Realtors Association, or the U.S. Forest Service).

- **Dictionaries.** Include foreign-language translation dictionaries.

- **Encyclopedias.**

- Other reference and supplementary reading materials.

The Audiovisual Center

Equipment and materials usually found in the audiovisual center include the following:

- **Cassette player with headphones.**

- **Videocassette recorder.**

- **Small television monitor.**

- **Follow-along books.**

- **Cassette tapes.** Separate these tapes into categories, such as music, bilingual/ESL, tapes about various subjects, stories on tape, and so on.

- **Videocassette tapes.** Your school district will probably supply you with educational tapes produced over public broadcasting, often furnished by the National Geographic Society. You will also want to stock a few tapes for their entertainment value, such as *Little House on the Prairie* and so on.

You should take two precautions if you decide to have an audiovisual center. First, carefully monitor any audio- or videotapes your students may smuggle into class, such as any selection by "Nasal Ned and His Nine Nasty Nose Pickers," and so on. Second, although some children are more knowledgeable than adults when it comes to electronic gadgetry, it's still a good idea to give them instruction in using and caring for the equipment.

The Science Center

The science center is a popular center, ideal for the kinesthetic learner who wants to experiment with a hands-on approach. This type of learner wants to figure out how things work, from pulleys, to fulcrums, to wheels and axles, to incline planes. Furnish your science center with as many of these items as possible:

- **Manipulatives.** Include things like wire, batteries, lightbulbs, tools, screws, incline planes, microscopes, magnets, thermometers, and harmless chemicals.

- **Books.** Assemble a library of science books with as broad a range of topics as possible. Such a collection should include pictures, activities, and experiments.

- **Photographs.** Furnish nature photographs as well as those relating to biology, physics, experiments, inventions, and so on.

- **Displays.** Create displays that demonstrate various scientific theories, as well as treasures your students have collected, such as rocks, bird's nests, and so on.

The Writing Center

The writing center will encourage your students to be creative by having fun with words. Include in the area a comfortable table and chair, along with a good reading lamp.

Furnish as many writing incentives as possible, including the following:

- Plenty of paper.

- Materials to use for illustrations, such as crayons, markers, and colored pencils.

- An idea file, including photos, Quick-Start Sheets (sheets of paper with a picture of a scene attached and a beginning sentence, such as "The boy in this picture is laughing because..."), and creative-writing kits.

The Math Center

The math center will be the favorite for many of your students; it's a spot where they can use manipulatives in solving math problems.

Here are some of the things you will need to furnish for the math center:

- Small objects for counting and weighing, such as buttons, rocks, bottle caps, beans, marbles, and so on.

- Materials for measuring, such as rulers, tape measures, string, yarn, and small boards.

- Materials for measuring temperature (thermometers).

- Objects for measuring time, such as a stopwatch, clock, and egg timer.

- Instruments for calculating, such as calculators and adding machines.

- Instruments for weighing, such as scales and balances.

Other helpful supplies include math games, play money, workbooks, graph paper, and plenty of plain paper.

The Pet Center

Here is another favorite spot, where you can keep your pet population. Your menagerie could include the following:

- Fish
- Snakes
- Guinea pigs
- Hamsters
- Rats
- Birds

Although pets require a lot of care, including feeding and cleaning their cages, they are an appreciated addition in any classroom. Many children don't have pets at home and are especially willing to help take care of those in your pet center. If you have guinea pigs or hamsters that reproduce during the school year, your students will have first-hand knowledge of this natural process. (By the way, the pet store will probably take the babies.)

You need to teach your students how to handle any pets, and you'll also need to watch the temperature in your room. Many pets can't survive if the room becomes too warm or cold, especially over weekends or school holidays. We can't tell you how many Christmas vacations we spent with some animal we brought home to live in our bathroom (so much for privacy).

We could write a whole chapter about our experiences with classroom pets throughout the years, but one stands out: A boy brought his pet snake to school one day, locked securely in its cage. A snake has 24 hours a day to figure how to get out of its cage, however, and this one did. It disappeared and was missing for three weeks. One day a girl sitting in a classroom four rooms down the hall let out a blood-curdling scream when she saw the snake peek out of a heating vent near her desk!

The Computer Center

If you're lucky, your classroom will be assigned at least one computer. This center requires a relatively small area, just enough room for a table, chair, the computer, and a box for disk or cassette storage. Hundreds of software programs are available to teach skills, word processing, programming, and problem-solving. Students will not only become familiar with computers in our electronic age (an important advantage), but they will be able to produce tangible work while learning. Take time to research available software; you'll find the computer center a helpful teaching aid for many of your subjects.

The Game Center

Although you can stock your game center with learning games, this area is often a reward-oriented activity center. This center usually has storage shelves and cabinets where you can keep your rainy-day classroom games, as well. Here are a few of the games you may want to furnish:

- Chess
- Checkers
- Puzzles
- Dominoes
- Scrabble
- Perquackey
- Crossword puzzles

Watch for store sales and garage sales that may have games at lower costs. If you purchase games at garage sales, however, make sure that all the pieces are there and that the games are in decent condition.

Watch for any students who demonstrate special ability in certain games; this may lead to an organized tournament. Sometimes a student who is poor academically will excel in chess, for example. For that student, winning is a terrific esteem-builder. This way, the student can shine in front of his or her peers.

Although interest centers take a lot of time and effort to facilitate, they are worth the trouble because children learn in different ways and these centers provide comfortable, relaxed opportunities for a variety of learning experiences. The centers also serve as motivators—sort of a carrot held out to students. If you have a student, for example, who doesn't usually do his homework, try this: "If you bring me your homework completed by tomorrow, you can have 15 minutes in any interest center you choose." This is an example of a contract you make with a student, and it's very effective.

 Note: See the helpful Web sites listed under "Resources" in the appendix for more creative ways to improve your classroom environment.

Conclusion

All in all, your classroom is your own world and you have control over its environment. Make your classroom as inviting and exciting as you can; you want your students to look forward to each school day, where they will not only learn, but also feel loved and nurtured.

Chapter 7

Teachers' Supplies

E very profession has its tools, and teaching is no exception. You need to outfit your desk, your filing cabinets, and your storage cabinets. You'll also need to decorate, as discussed in chapter 6.

Where does all this stuff come from? Some items are supplied through your school district's order catalog; some are available for free from various businesses and agencies; but some you will need to purchase yourself.

What You Will Need

This chapter provides you with lists of items you may want to consider having.

For Your Desk

- Two pairs of scissors
- Stapler
- Staples
- Staple remover
- Scotch tape
- Pens
- Pencils
- Paper clips
- Post-Its
- Notepads
- Note paper
- Kleenexes
- Bookends or a book rack (optional)
- Dictionary
- Lesson plan book

- Grade book
- Attendance book
- Desk pad (optional)
- Paperweights (optional)
- Huge paper clips or another type of giant clip
- Ruler
- Tools (pliers, screwdrivers, Allen wrench, hammer)
- Rubber bands
- Elmer's Glue
- A container for pens and pencils (optional)
- Desk-drawer organizers (optional)
- Correction fluid
- Art gum erasers
- Pink Pearl erasers
- School stationery and envelopes
- Thank-you notes and cards
- Postage stamps for personal notes
- Pencil compass
- School forms
- P.E. whistle (doesn't hurt to have two)
- Stopwatch (optional)
- Single-hole punch (optional)
- Safety pins of various sizes (you can't teach elementary school without them!)

For Your Filing Cabinet

- Hanging folders and manila folders
- Index tabs
- Binders and binder paper
- Plastic zipper bags or Zip-Loc bags
- Students' rewards and prizes

For Your Supply Cabinet

- String or yarn (for hanging things)
- Chalkboard erasers
- Chalk (or liquid writers, if appropriate)
- Chalk holders (optional)
- Cleaning supplies
- Art supplies

- Grade-appropriate paper, including handwriting paper
- Yardstick, meter stick, or pointer
- Chalkboard compass
- Push pins and straight pins
- Three-hole punch (optional)
- Masking tape
- Art supplies
- Paper cups
- Paper towels
- Bar soap
- Container or two of sawdust/meal used to absorb vomit (get a supply from your custodian)

- Hand broom and dust-pan (optional)
- Handcuffs (just kidding!)

Decorating/Teaching Supplies

- Bulletin board supplies
- Plants (optional)
- Animal cages (optional)
- Aquarium/terrarium (optional)
- Pull-down maps
- Globes
- Wall calendar
- Other decorative items needed to create your classroom environment (see chapter 6)

Supply Sources

The best source is your school district's supply catalog; you may be surprised at the things that are available when you ask for them.

Ask fellow teachers for their sources, especially if you're new to the district (they will know which local businesses have free goodies).

Here are some more sources:

- Garage sales and flea markets (hit these as soon as you can after you take a teaching position).

- Organizations that offer free or low-cost materials to teachers, such as those listed in the book *Free and Almost Free Things for Teachers* by Susan Osborn.

- Discount teacher-supply companies. One company in particular was formed by a group of teachers and offers surplus outlet materials at low cost. Their mail-order catalog is free upon request. Send a postcard to Creative Educational Surplus, 9801 James Circle, Bloomington, MN 55431.

- Web site suppliers (see "Resources" in the appendix).

- Retail teacher aid stores. Your local teacher aid supply store has thousands of tempting products for sale. If you've never been into one of these stores, allow plenty of time on your first visit because you'll be intrigued with the helpful materials available to you. You will probably find that your biggest outlay of expense will be during your first year of teaching, with the hope that you will be able to use most of your purchases over and over again.

Many teacher-supply stores will also furnish you with a catalog that you can look over at your leisure and place orders by mail. Here is a sample table of contents from one of these typical catalogs:

- New Products
- Audiovisual Equipment
- Furniture and Equipment
- Infant Furnishings
- Children's Books
- Storage Units and Accessories

- Early Childhood
  - *Creative Play Furnishings*
  - *Arts and Crafts*
  - *Active Play*
  - *Creative Play/Role Play*
  - *Manipulatives*
  - *Puzzles*

- ✎ *Perceptual Development*
- ✎ *Early Childhood Teacher Resource*
- Language Arts/Reading
- Cooperative Learning
- Social Studies
- Mathematics
- Science
- Gifted and Talented/ Critical Thinking
- Electronic Learning
- Music and Dance
- Crafts and Seasonal Activities
- Seasonal Decorations
- Bulletin Board Sets and Idea Books
- Flannel Board Activities
- Teacher Helpers
  - ✎ *Home and School Activities*
  - ✎ *Teacher Resource*

A catalog usually has about 300 pages. Here is a sample entry taken at random from the "Bulletin Board Sets" section:

Vertical Classroom Banners, die-cut banners extend to 11½" to 44" dimension. $2.65 each. Banners available:

EXPLORE WITH READING

WELCOME

WELCOME TO CLASS

HAPPY HOLIDAYS

NIGHT BEFORE CHRISTMAS

HAPPY VALENTINE'S DAY

HAPPY EASTER

Ready-made bulletin board materials are probably the most popular purchases for first-year teachers.

 Note: See "Resources" in the appendix for Web sites that offer teaching supplies, lesson plans, and decorating sources.

Conclusion

After you've taught for a few years, you'll accumulate reusable materials that will cut down on your out-of-pocket expenses each year. Your first year of teaching, however, will be your most expensive. The good news is that when all those relatives ask you what you want for Christmas, you'll definitely have a list!

Chapter 8

How to Prepare for a Substitute

Murphy's Law says that the day you wake up with chills, fever, and uncontrollable nausea will be the day you have absolutely nothing prepared for a substitute. Many teachers we interviewed said they have dragged themselves out of sickbeds to prepare for a sub. The garbage collector just calls in sick; the secretary calls in sick; and the custodian calls in sick. But with the teaching profession comes the responsibility of having to draw up detailed lesson plans, no matter how sick you are at the time.

Technically, your lesson plans should be complete, detailed, neatly written, and totally understandable to any individual. In practice, however, lesson plans can be rather sketchy, written as illegibly as a doctor's prescription, and understood only by the writer. If your plans are detailed and legible, you're probably pretty well set for a sub; however, if your lesson plans are brief notations, meaningful only to you, we suggest you have an emergency set of generic lesson plans available at all times. They should be clearly marked and should sit on top of your desk. In addition to these emergency plans, you also need a folder full of general information for the substitute.

Emergency Lesson Plans for Your Substitute

You should keep the emergency lesson plans in a brightly colored folder marked **LESSON PLANS FOR SUBSTITUTE** in bold letters across the top. This will help your sub find the folder easily. If you're seriously sick, you don't want to spend any more time on the phone than necessary explaining where to find the folder.

This substitute folder should contain supplementary lessons and activities relative to the subjects you are teaching that school year. Naturally, substitute lesson plans vary greatly from one teaching situation to another. You'll have one kind of lesson plan for a kindergarten class, for example, and an entirely different plan for fourth-graders. Whatever your grade level, the lessons and activities should have these characteristics in common:

- Directions that the sub and students can understand easily (concrete, not abstract)

- High success rate

- Should involve the students (with either verbal or hands-on work)

- Should be stimulating and have a high interest level

If you include worksheets, handouts, and so on, run them off ahead of time so that the sub will have one for each student without having to find the copy machine.

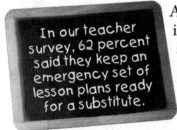

In our teacher survey, 62 percent said they keep an emergency set of lesson plans ready for a substitute.

Also inside the substitute folder, include extra sponge activities for the sub to use throughout the day. *Sponges* are short "filler" activities used to "soak up" a little extra time, such as the time between subjects or while waiting for the bell to ring.

Provide more than enough sponge activities (they may or may not relate to your academic subjects). There are literally hundreds of sponge ideas. Here are just a few:

- Sing a song.

- Count by fives to 200.

- Play "20 Questions" (have names of people, places, television shows, and so on for the students to guess).

- Take a word, such as *Thanksgiving,* and see how many words the students can make from the letters.

- Tell a story, having each child add a sentence until the story comes to an end. (Provide a couple of starter ideas to get things going.)

General Information for Your Substitute

In another folder boldly marked **GENERAL CLASS IN-FORMATION FOR SUBSTITUTE,** provide the following items:

- **Seating chart and class roster.** Include comments regarding any students who have special needs or problems.

- **Explanation of your discipline system.** If your discipline ladder includes writing names on the chalkboard followed by check marks, for example, explain your policy.

- **Fire-drill procedures.** Include a map that shows where your class is to be taken in case of a fire drill.

- **Class rules.** Provide a list of your class rules.

- **Map of the school.** Provide a map of your school and grounds; highlight and make notes marking any areas where the sub will be expected to serve duty, for example, "Recess duty in playground area No. 4."

- **Names of staff members.** Provide your sub with a list of any staff members the sub may need to call upon: the names of any teaching aides (including a list of their duties and the hours they come in to help), your "teaching buddy," if you have one, and all special teachers.

- **The name of your "student substitute helper."** Train one or two of your students to be the designated helpers for any substitute who teaches your class.

- **Substitute checklist.** Provide a form for the sub that includes your school's hours; your own schedule and times; all your regular duty assignments and times; and a list of general procedures regarding policies on snacks, lining up, bathroom use, lunchtime, and so on.

- **Substitute feedback form.** Provide a form that the sub can use to give you feedback, including which students were absent, which lesson plans were completed, any extra work that was done, any behavior problems, plus a space for general notes and comments.

- **Your home telephone number.**

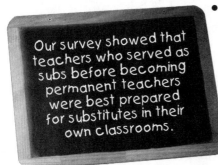

Our survey showed that teachers who served as subs before becoming permanent teachers were best prepared for substitutes in their own classrooms.

- **The names of students who are allowed to leave the classroom.** If you have students who are pulled out during the day for special classes or other approved reasons, leave a list, along with the days and times they are allowed to leave.

In the case of high-school students, you may also want to provide the names of the passes required, such as a band pass.

A Few Helpful Hints

When you're beginning a new job, it's hard to imagine planning for the day you'll be absent. The tips in this section are tried-and-true and based on our own experiences.

- **Enlist a teaching buddy.** Every teacher should have a teaching buddy, preferably one who teaches on the same team or grade level. Familiarize yourselves with each other's rooms, supplies, policies, students, discipline problems, and substitute folders. Put each other's names in your substitute folders so that your sub has someone handy to call in case of questions or confusion.

If you have a teaching buddy, you will have someone on hand in case of unusual circumstances, as well, such as a planned field trip, and so on. After all, Murphy's Law says you'll probably get sick on the day you're needed the most!

- **Make use of the substitute feedback forms.** After you've been gone, take some time to read over the feedback form. The responses will help you plan for subs in the future, but the form will also let you know which subs work out well with your class so that you can request them next time.

- **Be sure that the sub locks your classroom.** If your sub is required to turn off lights and lock your classroom door at the end of the day, be sure this is noted on the checklist in big red letters! Also, if the sub is to return the key to the secretary, to your box, or someplace else, be sure you spell this out very clearly. Not only will you be on the "bad side" of the custodians if this isn't done, but you may find things stolen from your classroom.

- **Anticipate discipline problems.** Don't leave this to chance. If you think your class may be unruly with a sub, make arrangements to have an administrator or your teaching buddy present to meet the sub at the beginning of the class. A brief visit of this type is usually enough to get the message across that bad behavior won't be tolerated. If you have a particular student you think may be a severe problem, alert your teaching buddy to be on call. Also, let the sub know that your teaching buddy is available if needed.

- **Beware of what you put in writing.** If you have certain students who have quirky social, discipline, or even

Be specific with your lesson plans, but don't be disappointed if your sub doesn't follow them exactly.

academic problems, be very careful what you put in writing. If you happen to have a sub who is a school parent, especially a parent of one of the children in your class, or who is a friend of a parent, you may be revealing something that can come back to haunt you!

Conclusion

We hope your subs always come prepared with their own bags of tricks, including their own academically challenging mini-lessons, fun games, creative art projects, and perhaps even a guitar to accompany group singing! In the real world, however, your sub will probably arrive with great expectations for the lesson plans you have provided. So, our advice to you is to join the 62 percent of the teachers in our survey who have emergency substitute plans on hand every day of the school year—assurance that you can be sick in peace!

Part III

The Big Three: Stress, Discipline, and Time Management

Chapter 9: Managing Your Stress

Chapter 10: Discipline and Classroom Control

Chapter 11: Time Management

Managing Your Stress

Teaching is a stressful profession—we already know that. What surprised us was the outcry of affirmation we received from the teachers we interviewed for this book. The stress out there is even worse than we thought.

Here are just a few of their complaints:

- "...too many meetings, not enough time to prepare."
- "...too many extra duties, parent conferences, Back-to-School Nights, Open Houses."
- "...six hours a day 'on stage' is exhausting!"
- "...not enough aide help."
- "...discipline problems are getting harder to handle all the time."
- "...problems with other staff members."
- "...overwhelming sense of responsibility—30 faces, 30 kids; am I fulfilling all their needs?"
- "...low salaries and job insecurity if nontenured."
- "...high expectations from parents and public in general."
- "...pressure to take classes at night in order to keep up my credentials."
- "...confrontations with angry parents."
- "...trying to be a teacher, mother, wife, cook, house-keeper, etc."

- "...need to find jobs during the summer to make ends meet."
- "...worried about how I'm being judged by my superiors."
- "...the job is never finished, even though I take work home at night."
- "...the enormity of the profession is overwhelming."

We could go on and on! In fact, if we took all of these stress factors, fed them into a computer, and asked for a solution, the computer would blow up! And it's no wonder, because in a recent study by the American Institute of Stress, school teaching was found to be the most stressful job in the nation, followed in order by these other professions:

- Police officer
- Air-traffic controller
- Miner
- Medical intern

Stress is a factor in more than two-thirds of visits to primary-care doctors.

Just think, teaching is three steps worse than an air-traffic controller, a profession notorious for its high burnout rate.

Stress can cause physical illness, depression, insomnia, marriage problems, and myriad other miserable conditions. Indeed, stress has become the emotional disease of the new millennium. Dr. Paul Rosch, head of the American Institute of Stress, says that stress gives us "a sense or feeling of being out of control," and that definitely applies to the teaching profession. It seems that as our list of responsibilities grows each teaching day, the number of available hours shrinks, until we feel pressed from every side.

Are there any answers? Fortunately, there are, and we want to share them in this chapter.

We have not only gleaned advice from nationally acclaimed professionals in the field of stress management, but from hundreds of fellow teachers who share ways they cope with this monster called stress.

EARLY WARNING SIGNS OF JOB STRESS
- Headache
- Sleep disturbances
- Difficulty concentrating
- Short temper
- Upset stomach
- Job dissatisfaction
- Low morale

—NIOSH, January 24, 2001
(The National Institute for Occupational Safety and Health)

Lighten Up!

This may sound like heresy, but don't take your job so seriously. Do you remember the teacher we told you about in the introduction to this book—the one who spent her evenings correcting papers and preparing for the next day? She wanted to spend her evenings with her husband and baby, but she never seemed to "get done." Even her weekends were tainted with guilt: "I should go over to the school and work for a few hours." She is typical of so many teachers, especially those who are new to the profession and haven't learned how to balance their jobs and personal lives. Notice that word: *job.* Teaching is, after all, a job, and you need to leave it behind you at the end of each day.

To keep stress from getting the best of you, you need to separate your professional life from your home life. Here are a few ways to do this:

- Learn to manage your time effectively. In chapter 11, we tackle the problem of time management, including ways to get better organized and cut down on the time it takes to grade papers, plan lessons, and put up bulletin boards. By using the ideas in that chapter, you can be home by 5 p.m. or earlier with no homework.

- Consider the possibility of a "shared-teaching" position.

- Seek out a mentor or veteran teacher who has learned how to separate his personal life from his teaching life. Ask for advice.

- Don't expect so much from yourself—you'll never get "done"! Lighten up and laugh a little!

- As you drive out of the school parking lot at the end of each day, resolve that you will not bore your spouse to death with the day's crises. Not only will your spouse appreciate this, but it will help you relax at the end of the day or over the weekend. The worst thing you can do during your time off is think about school and talk shop.

> It's not the load that breaks you down. It's the way you carry it.

- Cultivate friends outside the teaching profession; there is nothing quite as refreshing as an evening spent with stimulating, interesting people in other professions.

Relaxation Techniques

To reduce your chances of stress overload, you'll need to learn to relax. Here are teachers' favorite techniques:

- **Run away from home.** Our teacher survey found that "running away" is a favorite relaxation technique. Take a day or a weekend and make your escape. Sometimes it helps to get out of town because the excursion feels like a mini-vacation—you're not only away from home with its chores and responsibilities, but you're in a refreshing setting, away from anything familiar. And, best of all, you won't run into any of your students' parents! Your getaways don't have to be expensive; why not take a bike ride along a river path? Or how about a day at a free festival? Or an evening at a concert in the park? Read your newspaper's entertainment page and look for free stuff to do—there's plenty of it out there! Just be sure your destination is far enough away from your regular life to get your mind off teaching. If you book a hotel or motel for a weekend, look for one with a spa—you could use a whirlpool soak and a massage.

- **Take up a hobby.** Find something interesting to do in your free time—anything other than schoolwork! Every one of us has something we used to like to do before we became obsessed with our work. Many teachers we interviewed relax with hobbies such as crafting, theater work, gardening, playing a musical instrument, or even singing in a barbershop chorus. If you've let your profession gobble up your fun, think back to your "previous life" and try to remember what you looked forward to at the end of a day.

- **Relax at home.** Trying to relax in your own home is difficult because of all the distractions: laundry to be done, kitchen to be cleaned, garage to be swept, roses to be pruned, telephone to be answered, garbage to be emptied, and so on. Here are a few ideas to help you relax. They all require that you take the phone off the hook (or at least turn on your answering machine!).

  - *Soak in a hot bath along with some herbal bath oils while listening to relaxing music.*

  - *Read some good fiction.*

  - *Plan a romantic evening for you and your spouse, complete with candlelight, a fire in the fireplace, and your favorite music.*

  - *Schedule 30 minutes of quiet time; just relax and let your mind float.*

  - *Use muscle-relaxation techniques. One muscle-relaxation technique taught by psychologists and psychotherapists can be done easily at home. Darken the room, close your eyes, and slowly tense and release every muscle group in your body, from your scalp to your toes. You can do this while sitting or lying down. Simply take a deep breath and tense up any muscle group. If you tense up your face, for example, just close your eyes tight, grimace your mouth, and hold to the count of 30. Then let your breath out at the same time you relax those particular muscles. This relaxation technique may not sound like much, but once you've tried it, you'll be hooked. When you've made it all the way down your body, from head to toes, you'll feel so relaxed that you'll be sleepy. Obviously, this is also a way to cure insomnia. You can learn other relaxation techniques, as well, by taking classes or with how-to books and tapes.*

- **Treat yourself to a professional massage.** If you get really tense and find it impossible to relax, you may need an occasional full-body or upper-body massage. Look for a reputable therapist who is a member of the American Massage Therapy Association. (Write them at 1130 W. North Shore Ave., Chicago, IL 60626, or check their Web site at www.amtamassage.org, for names of therapists in your area.)

- **Sleep!** Recent studies done by sleep gurus have found that most Americans are suffering from sleep deprivation. If you aren't getting enough sleep, you're running on an empty tank, which means you don't have enough mental and physical strength to cope with each day's stress. The result is that small crises can become huge crises, and by the end of your teaching week you will feel drained. So, try adding an extra hour of sleep each night and, if possible, take a 10- or 20-minute catnap when you get home from school. This will rejuvenate you for the rest of the day.

Get Exercise Every Day

Exercise is another way to lower your stress level. Whether you take up a sport, exercise on your own, or just take a daily walk in the fresh air, exercise can help burn away the negative energy left over at the end of your day.

- **Be a sport!** In addition to taking up a hobby, how about joining a city-league softball team or trying golf or bowling? Or maybe you like to swim or play tennis. In any case, you need something that will take your mind off teaching and, preferably, get you into some fresh air.

You can't direct the wind, but you can adjust your sails.

- **Walk.** The experts tell us there is no better exercise than walking; it's free and makes no special demands on you. You don't need to drive anywhere and you don't need special exercise attire other than a sturdy pair of walking shoes. Walking is also convenient because you can walk out your front door whenever the mood hits you.

- **Exercise.** Whether you exercise at home or at a fitness club, you'll feel much better for it. Dr. Dean Ornish, a physician who directs the Preventive Medicine Research Institute in Sausalito, California, says that noncompetitive exercise is an amazingly effective stress reliever. He suggests moderate exercise for 20 or 30 minutes every day or one hour three times a week. In addition, he recommends frequent stretching exercises.

Eat Well

A healthy diet not only reduces stress, but improves your immune system at the same time! Keep these tips in mind as you examine your diet:

- **Beware of caffeine and chocolate.** Overindulging is natural when you're under stress, but try not to slurp down cup after cup of coffee, and try to substitute an apple for that Hershey bar! Try a relaxation technique instead.

- **Cut the fat.** Dr. Ornish says that you can eat all the carbohydrates and lean proteins you want as long as you keep fat to 10 percent of your daily calorie intake. One gram of fat has nine calories, so if you need 2,000 calories a day, your fat intake shouldn't exceed 200 calories $(2,000 \times 0.10 = 200)$ or 22 grams of fat $(200/9 = 22)$.

This means you'll need to eat more fruits and vegetables and less butter, cream, and fatty meats.

As a side benefit to healthy eating, another dietary expert, Henry T. Lynch, a researcher at the Creighton University School of Medicine, says that scientists now know for sure that a high-fiber, low-fat diet is a prudent precaution against cancer.

Keep a Positive Attitude and a Sense of Humor

Finding humor in a frustrating situation isn't easy; however, when things get tense, try to see the positive...and smile! Here are some practical ways to do this:

- **Hang out with positive, funny people.** Shed as many negative friends as you can and try to stay away from sour family members as well. Instead, spend more time with friends and family who are upbeat and have a sense of humor. By surrounding yourself with positive people, your own outlook will improve considerably. Nothing reduces stress like a good laugh!

- **Spread humor around your staff.** A psychotherapist named Jennie Holt instills humor on school campuses. She recently met with the elementary teachers at Chantilly School in Charlotte, North Carolina, who were in the process of reshaping their curriculum, finding ways to reach kids at different skill levels and from different cultural backgrounds.

  Dr. Holt discovered quickly that these teachers were completely stressed out. There was no laughter on staff—just difficult, serious, hard work. Her mission was to lighten things up around the place; get them laughing, joking, telling funny stories. She told them to clip jokes from magazines or comics from the newspaper and pin them up on the bulletin board. She encouraged them to look for things to laugh about and to share the laughter with each other. Chantilly

A smile uses only 13 muscles; a frown takes 64.

School now has a "joke bulletin board," a "joke of the month," a coffee hour before school, and a secret pals club. Chantilly's principal, Frances Waller, said that Dr. Holt's visit created a "very warm, caring environment."

- **Eliminate the negative.** Start monitoring what you say and think, substituting positive thoughts and words for negative ones. If you can't think of anything positive, don't say anything. The experts say that negatives breed negatives and positives breed positives. Therefore, if you want to feel better physically and mentally, try to be positive and upbeat, which in turn will reduce your anxiety and help you cope with daily stress.

Know When to Seek Professional Help

If your stress is out of control and none of our suggestions help, you may need professional help. How do you know whether you do? This section lists some of the red flags you should watch for.

Your Body

- Headaches
- Indigestion
- Dizziness
- Back pain
- Tension
- Racing heart

- Tightness in your neck and shoulders
- Tiredness
- Ringing in the ears
- Insomnia
- Sweaty palms

Your Behavior

- Compulsive gum-chewing
- Critical attitude toward others
- Grinding your teeth at night
- Compulsive eating

Your Emotions

- Crying
- Edginess
- Nervousness or anxiety

- Loneliness
- Overwhelming sense of pressure
- Anger
- Easily upset

Your Thoughts

- Forgetfulness
- Trouble thinking clearly
- Constant worry
- No sense of humor
- Inability to make decisions

If you have several of these symptoms and they seem to be forming a repetitive pattern, start getting a handle on your stress by visiting your medical doctor. If the doctor thinks your problem is more than physical, he or she may recommend a competent counselor.

 Note: For more help, see the "Support Groups" Web sites in the appendix.

Conclusion

One encouraging word: You don't need to eliminate stress from your life. After all, controlled stress is actually a creative, positive force. In fact, as far as we can determine, the only time you'll be completely free of stress is when you're lying still in your coffin.

Remember that although the teaching profession is a stressful one, you aren't alone. Many other professions are stressful as well. So do the best you can and remember that "it's just a job!" You also have a personal life, so don't be so hard on yourself. Take control of your stress and don't let it beat you!

Chapter 10

Discipline and Classroom Control

A fter many hours of work, your classroom finally has that certain "look" and "feel" and you're ready for your students! No matter how idyllic your classroom environment, however, it can turn sour very quickly unless you also have classroom control.

To be a successful teacher who enjoys the profession, you must have a positive discipline plan, not only for your sake, but for your students' sake as well. A learning environment free of disruptive behavior is not an easy goal to achieve. It is so difficult, in fact, that it is the number one reason teachers leave our profession.

Dozens of books have been written on this subject, including Lee Canter's popular *Assertive Discipline;* others are listed in the bibliography at the end of this book. Large bodies of research have been done on this aspect of teaching; however, our purpose in this chapter is to pass on some of the general principles and solutions we have found to work, along with excellent suggestions given by teachers who responded to our research survey.

Positive Reinforcements and Negative Consequences

A common thread among classroom discipline gurus is that behavior can be altered by using positive reinforcements and negative consequences. The idea is basically very simple:

1. There are rules.

2. Give positive recognition to students who abide by the rules.

3. Give negative consequences to students who do not abide by the rules.

The following suggestions and manner of speaking to the students will vary depending on grade level.

Classroom Rules

The first step is to decide which rules you want to establish for your classroom. (Your classroom rules are always in addition to general school rules, such as "No gum allowed," "Do not leave the school campus," and so on.) Keep your own classroom list to only five or six basic rules, such as these:

1. Do not leave the room without permission.

2. Raise your hand if you wish to speak.

3. Keep your hands and feet to yourself.

4. Use appropriate language.

5. Show respect for one another.

Positive Reinforcement

With positive reinforcement methods, such as praising your students, giving awards, and rewarding the class, you teach your class important lessons about discipline and boost their self-esteem in the process.

Praise

Look for ways to praise each student every day. Be sure the praise is sincere and tactful. By that we mean that some children respond to praise given in a quiet, individual way because they are embarrassed when praised in front of the class. Most children, however, thrive on "public praise," those affirmative strokes given in front of their peers. The shyer student will appreciate a comment as simple as "That's neat the way you did that." Shy children often have hidden insecurities, and your individual praise will alleviate many of them during the school year as you build their self-esteem. When you want to praise a child in front of the class, you might say something like this: "Beth has been working hard on her Valentine's card; hold it up for the class to see!"

Here are just a few actions or attitudes that deserve your praise:

- The class behaves well during an assembly or when a guest is in the room.
- A student raises his or her hand to speak.
- The class behaves well on a field trip.
- The class lines up quickly and quietly.
- A student helps pick up crayons another student has dropped.
- A student says, "Thank you."

Remember that every child needs strokes every day, no matter how well-adjusted he or she may seem. We feel so strongly about this, in fact, that we suggest you monitor the praise you give each day by keeping a list of your students, placing a check mark next to a student's name each time you give him or her strokes. This will ensure that you praise every child every day.

Awards
Students love to win awards, and each time they do, they receive positive reinforcement. Create awards appropriate to your grade level, such as Student of the Week and Student of the Month awards in grades four, five, and six, or clever good-behavior badges or bookmarks for the primary grades. Lee Canter's *Assertive Discipline Elementary Workbook* provides a couple dozen specific good-behavior badge and bookmark ideas to get you into the spirit of rewarding good behavior.

Rewards

In addition to individual awards, it's good to give group and class rewards. A small group may consist of four or five students. Some teachers give each group a name such as Team I or The Blue Team, and so on. The idea of small-group rewards is to encourage every member of the group to behave well because of peer pressure. If a class has one student who is such a disruptive discipline problem that no group wants that student on their team, the group reward idea usually won't work. In this case, it's better to reward the class as a whole. If you have only one disruptive student in your class, an alternative might be to move that particular student off by himself with the stipulation that he can move his desk up to join a group of his choice if he feels ready. If he becomes a problem for the group, the group itself won't be penalized. Rewards can range from class parties or special movies to free pencils, jelly beans, bookmarks, or even a designated amount of time a student may spend at the interest center of his or her choice.

Students can earn these rewards in a number of ways:

- **The marble jar.** We have found the marble jar to be a terrific motivator. You will need a medium-sized jar to hold the marbles (a two-gallon jug will take forever to fill!) and enough marbles to fill the jar. Place the jar in a visible spot. Whenever a student or the class earns a marble, drop it into the jar with as much ceremony as possible. Individual students can earn marbles for such things as helping another child or completing homework on time. The class as a whole can earn marbles by working well together, behaving on a field trip, or lining up quietly. (You'll find that "lining up" is one of the "loftiest" skills you can teach your children because we seem to spend most of our lives in one form of line or another—at the grocery store, at the bank, in the military, waiting for theater tickets, and so on.) When the marble jar is full, the reward is usually a fun class activity, such as throwing an ice-cream or pizza party, watching a special video, or a free hour on the playground (with your principal's permission, of course).

- **Spending money.** Many teachers use some version of free "bucks" that are given to students as a reward for positive behavior or achievement. These bucks may look something like this:

Students accumulate the bucks to spend on little prizes (special pencils, jelly beans, felt-tip markers, candy bars, rulers, free books from your book club, individual time to spend at an interest center, and so on). Or you may want to organize an auction (remember chapter 4?) where your students can use their bucks to bid on prizes.

Phone Calls and Notes to Parents

Another effective motivator is positive contact with the parents of a child who has been behaving well. This may sound like a time-consuming bother, but it's worth it. You not only build positive rapport with the parents, but you will find that students' behavior will improve greatly on the hope of a call or note home. Most children want to please their parents, and a positive report mysteriously results in more positive behavior, which requires more notes and phone calls, and on and on. Try this idea and you'll see results. You'll spend minutes but save hours.

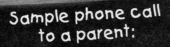

Sample phone call to a parent:

"Hello, Mrs. Smith? This is Mr. Thompson, Jimmy's teacher. I just want you to know how pleased I am with his behavior so far this year. He's doing a great job!"

Negative Consequences

Wouldn't it be great if all students would respond well to positive reinforcement? Unfortunately, you will have a few students who disrupt your class with negative behavior. This is why you need a specific preplanned classroom "discipline ladder" (also known as a *discipline hierarchy*). There are many types of discipline ladders, but they all seem to have one thing in common: Small offenses result in small consequences and major offenses result in major consequences. Average offenses, of course, fall somewhere in the middle. The important thing to remember is that once you have decided on your own discipline ladder, you must be consistent in its use. For example, at the bottom of your ladder you may give only a verbal warning for a small offense such as yelling out an answer without raising a hand. At the top of your ladder, the consequence for a more serious offense may be a trip to the principal as well as contact with the parents. An example of a serious offense may be a student physically attacking another student.

A Sample Discipline Ladder

There are dozens of discipline ladders, but here is one that has worked well for us:

1. Write the student's name on the board (this is a warning).

2. Put one check beside the student's name (usually results in detention time).

3. Put a second check beside the student's name (also results in detention time).

4. A private talk with the student.

5. Contact with the parent.

6. Contact with the principal.

7. Conference with the parent, principal, and student.

8. Suspension from school.

 Note: Follow your school's discipline policy regarding school suspension. Also, be aware that any discipline problems you may have with a Special Ed student are usually not handled with a discipline ladder, but are instead referred to the child's Special Ed teacher for special handling.

Alternative Methods of Classroom Control

Here are some other ideas you might want to try:

- **Time-Out.** A time-out is exactly what it sounds like—a way to remove a disruptive student from the rest of the class. Time-out works especially well for elementary students, from a time-out chair in the primary grades to a time-out table for the upper grades. It's important that you limit the time-out period to a realistic length—maybe a maximum of 10 or 15 minutes.

- **"The Look."** Many teachers get results by making eye contact with a disruptive student. This visual communication should say, "I notice your behavior and I want you to change it immediately!" Don't discount this simple action—eye contact is a powerful tool.

- **"The Walk."** This is another effective way to stop disruptive behavior. While continuing to teach, begin "the walk," stopping beside the student who is misbehaving. Stand next to the student or even place your hand on the student's shoulder in an unobtrusive way until the behavior stops.

Note: "The Look" and "the Walk" prevent a student from disrupting your teaching rhythm. Every time a disruptive student robs you of one minute of time, you have actually lost 30 minutes of instruction when multiplied by 30 students.

- **One-on-one talk.** As unlikely as it may sound, it often works to take a disruptive student aside (at recess or after school) for a one-on-one talk. Pull up a chair, sit down, and explain to the student why his or her behavior is unacceptable. You might say something like this: "You know, you're making my job much more difficult than it needs to be." Make the student feel you're dealing fairly without lowering your standards. The student will sense a caring relationship developing, a building of rapport. The key to a one-on-one talk is to convince the student you like him or her—but not the bad behavior.

- **Use humor to defuse a potential problem.** Humor comes in handy throughout the teaching day, but it is especially useful as a deterrent to problems before they fully develop. For example, you may have a couple of boys who are crossways with each other and threaten to "beat each other up" at recess. You may say something like this (in an animated way): "Hey, you don't want to beat up a nice kid like Alan, do you?" Or if a student overreacts and "tattles" on another student who used her pencil, say, "Oh, no! Not your pencil! I'd sure be mad if someone used my pencil!"

- **Let the student decide his or her own fate.** When you have a student who continually disrupts the class, you may find it worthwhile to ask the student this question: "How do you think we should handle the problem?" Then offer three options and let the student choose one. By giving her a choice, you may find she is harder on herself than you would have been. And once the student has made her choice, she has, in effect, agreed to abide by it.

- **Signed contract.** If you have a problem student who has not responded to anything else, draw up a formal contract for him or her to sign. This contract usually includes the date, your name, the student's name, behavior changes he or she agrees to make and, finally, a place for the student's signature. It is a good idea to have the student sign this contract at a parent-teacher conference, not only in your presence, but also in the presence of the parents as well.

- **The parent monitor.** If you want to put holy fear into your students, threaten to have one of their parents monitor their behavior for a whole day in the classroom. The most humiliating and embarrassing punishment a student can think of is to have his mother sit next to him in class all day. In fact, if you enforce this threat even one time with one student, it will be an effective deterrent for the whole class the rest of the school year! Obviously, you need to work out this arrangement with the parent in advance, and both you and the parent must be willing to follow through. The parent must also adopt a serious "I'm-here-to-see-how-bad-your-behavior-is" attitude and should be polite, but not particularly friendly, to the child. This is not to be construed as a friendly visit.

Severe Discipline Problems

Unfortunately, the new millennium is synonymous with vulgar language, violence, drugs, alcohol, vandalism, stealing, gangs, weapons, and inappropriate sexual behavior. Although we tend to see these problems more among middle-school and high-school students, elementary children aren't immune to any of this behavior.

Teachers in 1996 said for the first time that discipline is the main reason teachers leave the profession.

—The Third Phi Delta Kappa Poll of Teachers' Attitudes Toward Public School, Phi Delta Kappan, 1996.

Vulgar Language

Standards have obviously changed through the years. What was once considered a dirty word when we started teaching is now flaunted by radio, television, movies, and in society as a whole. One example might be the word *bitchin'*. Although this word has evolved in society from an insult to a slang compliment, that still doesn't necessarily make it an acceptable term on your school campus. Many other terms that were once forbidden are now used indiscriminately, not only by students, but teachers as well. One teacher was so appalled at a student who was spitting on her classroom windows that she yelled: "Knock that sh– off!" The student went directly to the vice principal and complained that the teacher "swore at me." This put the vice principal on the spot because the expletive was a word not allowed to be used on his campus by anyone.

Obviously, this is a gray area in school discipline that has become a philosophical issue. Our feeling is that a school is a sanctuary from the rest of the child's world; even if the child is inundated with foul language in the home, the school should maintain higher standards. Therefore, as you establish standards to be upheld in your own classroom, you need to weigh several things: the standards already set by your school administration; the social morals of your community; the potential for support from your administration; and your own personal moral and social standards.

Note: On a multicultural campus, students sometimes swear in their own language. In fact, they may even throw vulgar insults at you, knowing you can't understand them. Learn to recognize these words.

Sexual Misbehavior

Sexual misbehavior can begin in the elementary grades when a boy sneaks up and snaps a fourth-grade girl's training bra or teases an especially well-developed fifth-grader. By the time the students reach middle school and high school, they have seen, read, or heard just about everything, with the help of television, books, movies, and popular music.

As you set your own classroom standards, make sure they correlate with your school rules. Remember that you have the right to forbid any offensive behavior in your classroom. Many junior and senior high schools draw the line at necking, kissing, or petting, although holding hands is fine. Whenever you find a school that has a lax policy, or no rules at all, you will find that the students take their "sexual freedom" as far as possible. Any behavior that embarrasses or offends others should not be allowed on campus.

Stealing

Stealing also has become commonplace on all campuses, from elementary to high school. Obviously, the thefts vary in their degree of seriousness and the way they should be handled. On the elementary level, students may steal everything from crayons to lunch money. Older students have more expensive tastes, from clothes to jewelry to cars. Students steal for many reasons: for attention; because they are kleptomaniacs; because they're jealous of another student's expensive possession; because they feel they have the right "to take" from those who "have"; because they need the money; or because they want a "thrill ride."

On the elementary level, you never know for sure whether a student is guilty unless you actually see the theft take place or the thief confesses. Usually on the first offense, a teacher has a talk with the guilty student. However, if the same student continually steals from you or others in the class, you will need to take the more serious steps on your discipline ladder. Occasionally, you will suspect that a child actually is afflicted with kleptomania and may need to be referred for professional help.

If you did not witness a theft, but you know who did it, one effective approach is to say, "It appears you took it; you're the only one who knows for sure. We can settle it now, or we can call the authorities and let them investigate." In the case of an elementary-school student, you would probably threaten to call the principal; in the case of an older student, you may threaten to call the police. This almost always brings a confession, especially from a high-school student.

Then there's the case of the "proud thief" who steals in the hope everyone will know. This pathetic character is starved for attention and wants to get caught.

Some students wear very expensive clothing to school; they also bring along enviable accessories and school supplies. These students are in real jeopardy of having something stolen by the "have nots," who justify their thefts because "it's not fair for some kids to have great stuff when the rest of us can't afford it." An extreme case involved a jealous girl who not only stole another girl's new leather coat, but really took out her wrath by defecating on it in the restroom. In a case like this—or one involving the theft of a student's watch, money, or other possession—refer the student to your school's administration immediately. If you suspect or you have been told that a stolen item has been hidden somewhere on campus, such as in a locker or desk, you should know that, in most states, your administrator has the right to make a search without a search warrant.

Car thefts are another problem on many campuses and should be reported to the school administration; however, a major theft usually becomes a criminal case as soon as its owner files a police report.

Here are a few measures that you can take to prevent thefts from happening on school campuses:

- Discourage students from bringing expensive, easily stolen items to school in the first place. (Advise parents of this policy and solicit their support.)

- Lock up your purse or any money that you've collected. (Your desk should have at least one security drawer.)

- Watch for any suspicious activities on your campus, especially older students (perhaps from a nearby middle school or high school) walking through your campus on their way home.

- Don't leave any valuable personal items in your room overnight, such as a musical instrument.

- Don't leave purses or valuables in plain view in a parked car, especially during an evening meeting at your school.

- Encourage your students to take all clothing and personal property home with them each day.

- Never allow students to go through anyone's desk, including yours.

- Don't allow students to trade toys or sell items to each other. (This often results in excuses like "he gave it to me" or "I found it," and so on.)

- Tell your students not to leave valuables in their lockers. (Lockers may seem secure, but are actually quite easy to break into.)

Drugs and Alcohol

We're finally out of the gray areas and into one that is definitely black and white. If you have any suspicion that a student is in possession of or has been using drugs or alcohol on campus, send for an administrator immediately, but don't let the suspected student out of your sight! (It's too easy for the student to stash or trash the drugs or alcohol on the way to the office.) Watch for changes in students' behavior, listen when you overhear any conversations that implicate a student, and don't be naive to the use of drugs and alcohol on your campus.

> 76 percent of high-school students and 46 percent of middle-school students say drugs are kept, used, or sold on school grounds.
>
> —Center on Addiction and Substantive Abuse, 1997

About three million crimes occur on or near school property each year. A reported 135,000 students carry guns to school every day.

—National Association of Secondary School Principals, 1998

A history teacher at one high school never seemed to catch on to the fact that several boys were drunk in one of his classes. The class was the first period after lunch and several boys habitually drank vodka mixed with a soft drink over the lunch period—not because they liked it, but because it was a "cool" thing to do. The drink had no alcohol smell, but the boys' behavior should have given them away.

Weapons

It is a serious offense for a student to be found using or carrying a weapon on a school campus. In fact, the law is so strict in some cities and states that it may result in expulsion from school. If you realize a student has a weapon in his possession, either send a student for an administrator or call for one over your intercom. Unless you feel that it is totally safe to do so, never try to disarm a student yourself. Stay cool and calm and wait for the arrival of an administrator who is trained to handle this type of offense.

You may think that your school is exempt from this type of danger; however, a recent Justice Department survey of 10 inner-city high schools in the state of Washington reported that 22 percent of the 758 male students questioned possessed guns. An alarming number of elementary-age students have been found with weapons, too. The problem is growing, so don't live in a dream world: Be aware and watch for weapons.

Gangs

Find out what your school administration policy is in regard to gang activity. This policy should be no secret to staff members; in fact, you will probably be sent for in-service training on this subject. Find out the exact procedures you are to follow if you suspect gang activities on campus. Your school may even have a dress code that prohibits gang-related attire. In any case, this is another serious problem in many of our schools and you need to know exactly how your administration expects you to handle it.

Violence

Students who exhibit violent behavior may do so for various reasons. Some may have serious emotional problems that cause them to become volatile or combative. This type of student can benefit from referral to professional help; however, there is sometimes a parent involved who is in a state of denial over the child's behavior and may not think the child needs professional help or medication.

Violence also shows up in the form of fights, as retaliation between gang members to "pay back" another student for something one gang member did, or as retaliation between individual students. These fights range from simple "scraps" on the elementary-school play-ground to knife or gun fights among high-schoolers. When we talk about serious fights, we don't always mean boys. When two girls get into a fight, it can be like trying to separate barbed wire; you've never seen such biting, grabbing, swearing, and hair-pulling. A fight that becomes an explosive situation needs to be handled with extreme caution.

6,093 students were expelled during the 1996–1997 academic year for bringing firearms or explosives to school.

—Department of Education, 1998

Here are some words of advice from experts trained to handle violent encounters:

1. Say "Stop!" or "Knock it off!" in a firm voice. If this doesn't work, go to the next step.

2. Send another student for an administrator.

3. Never try to overpower a violent student.

4. Don't stand directly in front of a violent student (stand to the side when speaking to him or her). When you stand directly in front of the student, you become the confronter.

5. Avoid touching a violent student.

6. Buy time, if possible, by trying to get the student(s) to sit down and talk with you. (If either student will talk, keep him or her talking until help arrives.)

7. Do not raise your voice or offer ultimatums.

8. Watch your back: Knives and guns have a way of appearing at the site of a fight.

9. Be prepared to write a detailed report of the incident, if required by your administration, including names, date, and a description of what happened as you saw it.

One in five parents reported his or her child had seen a firearm or other weapon in school or the community.

—1999 National Crime Prevention Survey

If Step 1 works and the combatants stop fighting upon your command to stop, it's important to isolate these combatants from the crowd that may have gathered. Give both students a chance to save face by getting away from their peers, who may be fueling the fire. Once the students are away from their audience, try to find out what caused the fight and get them talking about it, which may even result in an apology.

"Keep Schools Safe" Violence Prevention

In the wake of the Columbine tragedy in Colorado and similar incidents in other states, including Oklahoma, Georgia, Tennessee, Arkansas, Kentucky, California, and Washington, agencies across the country have taken action to prevent school violence.

We all recall that heart-wrenching day on April 20, 1999, when two students took the lives of 15 people at Columbine High School in Littleton, Colorado. That devastating tragedy has resulted in hundreds of unprecedented new safeguards being put into effect. Not only have school districts issued new security guidelines, but teachers have been attending in-service training on the subjects of prevention, intervention, and crisis control. You have probably attended similar classes offered by your district where you have learned a new set of rules entirely for preventing and dealing with extreme acts of violence—and God forbid one should ever take place in your school.

One violence-prevention organization, known as Keep Schools Safe, is a joint project of the National Association of Attorneys General and the National School Boards Association. If you check out their Web site at www.keepschoolssafe.org, you'll find dozens of articles that will help you deal with this problem, including how to detect the warning signs of a potentially violent student.

One of their articles, "School Safety: Working Together to Keep Schools Safe," includes this helpful list of general warning signs:

- A history of violence
- A close family member who has committed a violent act
- A history of alcohol or drug abuse
- A precipitating event, such as a failed romance or the perception of a failure
- The availability of a weapon or the means to commit violence
- A recent attempt to commit suicide or an act of violence
- A lack of coping skills or strategies to handle personal life crises with no controls to prevent anger or positive ways to release it
- No apparent emotional support system
- A lack of involvement in extracurricular activities

Another interesting list from the FBI *Law Enforcement Bulletin,* September 1999, gives common characteristics of some school shooters. Although these behaviors should not be, by themselves, thought of as the causes of violence, they were observed and reported to be conditions or behaviors commonly found in the students studied.

- The suspects were white males under 18 years old with mass or spree murder traits.

- They sought to defend narcissistic views or favorable beliefs about themselves, while at the same time they had very low self-esteem.

- They experienced a precipitating event that resulted in depression and suicidal thoughts that turned homicidal.

- They lacked, or perceived a lack of, family support.

- They felt rejected by others and sought revenge or retaliation for real or perceived wrongs done to them.

- They acquired firearms generally owned by a family member or someone they knew.

- They perceived that they were different from others and disliked those who were different. They needed recognition, and when they did not receive positive recognition, they sought negative recognition.

- They had a history of expressing anger or displaying minor acts of aggressive physical contact at school.

- They had a history of mental health treatment.

- They seemed to have trouble with their parents, though no apparent evidence of parental abuse existed.

- They were influenced by satanic or cult-type belief systems or philosophical works.

- They listened to songs that promote violence.

- They appeared to be loners, average students, and sloppy or unkempt in dress.

- They seemed to be influenced or used by other manipulative students to commit extreme acts of violence.

- They appeared isolated from others, seeking notoriety by attempting to "copycat" other previous school shootings, but wanting to do it better than the last shooter.

- They had a propensity to dislike popular students or students who bully others.

- They expressed interest in previous killings.

- They felt powerless and, to this end, may have committed acts of violence to assert power over others.

- They openly expressed a desire to kill others.

- They exhibited no remorse after the killings.

Fortunately, in spite of the vast media publicity these tragedies generate, this type of incident is rare. Although we don't recommend you dwell on school violence, you as a teacher need to be aware of these characteristics so that you can possibly spot potentially violent students at your school.

For more information on how to prevent school violence, we have included a comprehensive list of Web sites in the appendix at the back of this book. One interesting site, for example, is the *Denver Post* Web site (www.denverpost.com), where you can read in great detail the reports, testimonies, and articles pertaining to the Columbine tragedy (click on "Columbine"). The profiles of the two shooters are included, as well as warning signs that, according to many, should have been recognized ahead of time. It's interesting that one warning sign was noted ahead of time by a teacher who became alarmed by the violence depicted in an essay written by one of the killers.

Caution: Many experts are advising teachers not to jump to conclusions; if a student exhibits one or more of the characteristics listed above, you should pass along word to your administrator or school counselor. Don't try to handle it yourself. Teachers are not trained psychologists. It is up to trained professionals to determine whether a child has violent tendencies. Meanwhile, it is wise for you to be aware of the warning signs.

Conclusion

In conclusion, here are a few words of general advice:

- You have the right to uphold your standards and to expect a comfortable, controlled classroom.

- Be consistent.

- Keep your sense of humor!

- Never argue with a student; to do so is to lower yourself to his level. You seldom, if ever, win an argument with a student.

- Your students will respect you if:

  - *your expectations are realistic;*
  - *you are firm, but fair; and*
  - *you let them know you care for them.*

- Don't be afraid to ask fellow teachers for advice, especially veteran teachers who have had experience dealing with discipline problems in your school. If you're lucky, your district may provide you with a mentor teacher.

As we conclude this chapter, we want to leave you with this word of encouragement: Each one of you, no matter what your size, age, or gender, can learn to be firm, assertive, and effective when it comes to discipline and classroom control. Good discipline takes effort and commitment, but you didn't get where you are without effort and commitment. We hate to see good people leave the profession because of their inability to handle discipline and classroom control.

Chapter 11

Time Management

I t isn't only the teaching profession that has become more complicated–life has become more complicated! That's why we need to manage our time efficiently. Otherwise, the 21st century will bury us under its increased load of responsibilities.

As we conducted our research for this book, we found that most of the teachers we interviewed are drowning in busy-work; very few ever feel "done." Our goal in this chapter is to show you how wise time management can help you feel "done" at the end of each day. We want you to be able to go home and enjoy your evening or weekend in peace.

The three keys to managing your time are

- Prioritization
- Organization
- Setting goals

The following sections detail each of these basic pieces of time management.

Learn to Prioritize

A teacher at one school (maybe you can identify with her) grades papers every available minute–during breaks, over lunch, and during teacher staff meetings and assemblies. (We aren't sure whether she takes them into the restroom with her, but we feel it is a distinct possibility.) Then, at the end of each frenzied day, she still is so loaded down with tote bags of work that she can hardly carry it all to her car. Not only does she correct way too many papers, but she spends too much time each evening making out elaborate, detailed lesson plans for the next day. She doesn't realize it, but she's heading for total burnout in a few more years!

We believe every teacher should be able to assess students' work and plan effective lesson plans within a routine schedule at school. You can work out a realistic schedule for yourself each day that allows time for paper grading and planning and still be able to leave at a reasonable hour with no extra "home" work. For example, if your school day begins at 8:30 a.m. and ends at 3:30 p.m., your work day may go from 7:30 a.m. to 4:30 p.m., which gives you two hours each day to evaluate and prepare for the next day.

This is in contrast to some teachers who arrive just in the nick of time in the morning and leave as soon as the "law" allows in the afternoon, which usually results in them taking home armloads of work at night. Doesn't it make sense to put in your prep time during a couple of extra hours at school? Then you can go home, relax, and enjoy your personal time away from school.

Of course, you don't always get this two-hour time period every day, as we know, because of staff meetings, committee meetings, professional growth classes, and so on. What we're suggesting is that you at least allot this time and be as consistent with it as you can. We've tried it both ways and we definitely prefer getting as much done at school as we can within a realistic time frame and then going home for the evening.

It goes without saying that there will be times when you must get away earlier for one reason or another. Perhaps you have a prescheduled appointment, such as a visit to your doctor or dentist. Or maybe you need to pick up your children from day care or a baby-sitter every day. This puts a real crimp in your time management because it probably means bringing home work pretty often.

To help you with your time management in general and this two-hour planning time more specifically, the following sections explain a few suggestions for streamlining the time you spend evaluating and planning:

Ask Your Teaching Aide to Help Grade Papers and Tests

If you are lucky enough to have an aide, be sure any of his or her "dead time" is spent grading, especially the papers that require only objective evaluation.

Correct Every Third Paper

Instead of correcting every single homework paper, writing sample, and so on, correct only every third paper for each student. Require the same amount of work from your students, skim over two of the papers, but correct the third in detail. This is an efficient, yet accurate, assessment of a student's work; save the graded work in the student's portfolio.

Do Brief Assessments of Written Essay Compositions

Written compositions are the most time-consuming to correct; however, your goal is to assess whether your students understand key points you have been teaching, such as in the development of a paragraph, for example. Is there a logical beginning and end and a flowing sequence of ideas in between? You can assess all these points briefly, without reading the entire composition every time.

Use the "Circle Your Best 10 Lines" Method of Grading

Have your students read their compositions carefully, circling their favorite block of 10 consecutive lines of writing. This is the only block of writing you will grade in this particular assignment. You haven't required less writing from each student, but you have saved yourself hours of reading and correcting without losing integrity in your grading.

Use Volunteers to Help Grade

Solicit the help of parents, senior citizens, or student aides who are willing to stay after school (especially in the upper grades). This type of volunteer help usually works out best when you have a "key" for easy grading.

Use Alternative Methods of Authentic Assessment

Instead of giving a written test to evaluate your students' knowledge of subject matter, use alternative methods. For example, if you're teaching the Westward Movement, have your students draw a mural that shows what they have learned.

Make Quality Lesson Plans in Less Time

This is something that comes with years of teaching experience; however, new teachers also can learn to plan well-designed lessons in less time. By the time you graduate and start your teaching career, you have been totally immersed in the five-point lesson plan. In fact, you've turned in most of these plans for critique and course credit. What most professors don't explain is that in the real world of teaching, you don't have several hours each day to prepare the next day's lessons. They also neglect to mention that an excellent lesson plan may not necessarily be a work of art. Unless your administrator regularly examines your lesson plans, it doesn't hurt to make them brief, using your own form of shorthand. The important thing is that your lesson plans result in effective teaching. Believe us, we've seen many fancy lesson plans prepared by ineffective teachers.

A professor of Education at the University of Northern Colorado challenged his class of master's degree students with this: "Give me a math objective, appropriate for your grade level, and I'll make a lesson plan on the spot for you." One student suggested "How to Find the Diameter of a Circle." The professor wrote a great, teachable lesson plan, using all the components of teaching a behavioral objective, and he did it in about five minutes. He obviously knew what he was doing, but the point is that lesson planning can be done informally and quickly and still be effective.

One word of advice: Take time before your school year begins to outline all your plans in a general way; this will give you a head start as you prepare weekly lesson plans once you're in the throes of teaching. You can write and implement more specific daily plans during the week as necessary.

Don't Let Bulletin Boards Consume Your Extra Time

Keeping your bulletin boards fresh and in season can really consume your precious time. Here are a few ways to cut down on "bulletin board hours":

- **Don't get so fancy!** Especially your first year or two, when you're breaking into teaching, avoid elaborate displays.

- **Let your teaching aide help.** If you are lucky, your aide will be talented in this way.

- **Let your students help.** You'll probably have at least one or two students each year who love to help with room decorations. You can post a bulletin board sign-up sheet to give all interested students a chance.

- **Buy ready-to-use bulletin board displays from your teaching-aid supply stores.** They are worth the investment and can be used again over several years.

- **Use a letter punch.** If your school or district provides a letter punch, be sure to use it! It will save you hours of cutting!

- **Donate one eight-hour day from each of your Christmas and spring breaks to work on bulletin boards.** You'll be surprised how much you can get done in eight uninterrupted hours! During Christmas break, for example, you can take down all your Christmas displays, put up your January boards, and have time left over for general housekeeping and to assess your teaching goals to date.

Learn to Organize

Time-management experts say that you'll waste less time if you're organized, and we've all heard that we waste a fourth of our lives looking for things. If there's any profession that's hurting for spare time, it's the teaching profession—which means that you need to get organized. Here are some areas that you can organize:

Your Desk

The efficiency experts also say that the more clear space you have on top of your desk, the more efficient you'll be. A teacher's desk can become cluttered very easily, so try to keep all your desk supplies hidden away in the drawers, except for the following things:

- One book holder for frequently used books (dictionary, grade book, the current book used in your literature curriculum, teacher editions of textbooks, and so on)
- Stapler
- In/out baskets
- Cup for pens and pencils
- Desk or flip calendar

Filing Cabinet

A well-organized filing cabinet usually has hanging folders with color-coded dividers. Here are some typical filing categories:

- Correspondence
- In-service notes

- Field trips (brochures, permission forms, and so on)

- District information (school calendar, handbooks, school and district policies, and so on)

- Personal (a copy of your teaching contract, a copy of the salary schedule, insurance benefits, and so on)

- Organizations (NEA, state and local teaching chapters, PTA, and so on)

- Faculty meetings

- Committees

- Audiovisual (catalogs, order forms, and so on)

- Standardized testing materials

- Report card forms

- Parent-teacher conference forms

- Sections according to subject, including lesson plans. (Keep these sorted as you go along by keeping lessons that worked and tossing those that didn't, along with any outdated materials.)

- Tickler file. (This is a file in which you keep "things to do" in order by the date you should do them. The key is to look in this file every morning!)

Reminder notes on your desk will help, too.

Storage Cabinets

You need to keep your storage cabinets neatly organized so that you can put your hand on anything as you need it. Hopefully, your cabinet will have drawers or shelves for paper and other items. Here are materials typically found in a classroom storage cabinet:

- Items too large for your filing cabinet that relate to subjects within it.

- Large, flat items (bulletin board supplies, posters, charts, photos, and so on)

- Construction paper, newsprint, graph paper, lined paper, and so on. (When you get paper from your school supply room, tear off the end of the package so that you can see what it is without removing all the paper from the package.)

- Art/science supplies

Your Calendar

If you're going to stay organized and never be surprised by something you should have done, you need a color-coded calendar. You can use the desk pad type (some teachers mount these under plastic or glass on their desk) or a wall calendar.

The first priority is that this calendar contain all the dates from your school calendar (write these dates on your home calendar as well). You also need to enter any dates peculiar to your own classroom or grade level, such as an upcoming field trip (mark the date permission slips are to go home with the students, the date they are due back to you, and so on). Use your tickler file in conjunction with the calendar so that your field trip forms, for example, coordinate with the same dates on each.

By the way, in addition to recording your school schedule and deadlines on your home calendar, you should also transfer important entries from your home calendar to your school calendar. That way you won't accidentally schedule a parent conference the afternoon you promised to take your son to soccer practice!

Learn to Set Goals

You can save a lot of time personally and professionally by sitting down once in a while to figure out where you've been and where you're going. This process will result in a better balance in your life, more time for yourself and your family, and a less harried, frenzied feeling all day long.

By setting short-term and long-term goals and then analyzing your progress from time to time, you will have a handle on what's working and what isn't. Without this introspection, you may inadvertently continue to waste time on things that aren't working for you at all.

An example of a long-term goal may be to eventually earn an administrative degree; you can accomplish this only by meeting short-term goals such as taking two three-unit courses each year. Or, perhaps you have a long-term goal of losing a certain amount of weight; this will happen only if you set short-term goals, such as walking during your lunch break, which may also give you more patience and energy for the rest of the day.

Conclusion

By learning to prioritize, organize, and set goals, you can add many valuable hours to each work week and still have time left over for some fun! We want your teaching career to last as long as *you* want; we don't want you to burn out because you manage your time poorly. As a brand-new teacher, you expect much of yourself, but you need to realize that there aren't enough hours in a day to meet the lofty standards you have probably set. So, do the best you can in the time available, and then go home and enjoy your personal life!

Part IV

Words of Encouragement

Chapter 12

Ask the Old Pros

A s we conducted our survey for this book, we asked teachers to supply questions for this chapter. We chose the tough questions, the ones most teachers seem to be asking. We have answered these questions as honestly as we can, and we hope you will benefit from our years of experience.

Teaching Issues

Q: *Should you attempt to cover the whole curriculum?*

A: The key word in this question is *cover.* I prefer the word *teach.* The curriculum you are expected to teach each year is rather static. The group of children you are expected to teach can vary greatly from year to year. One year you might accomplish teaching practically the entire curriculum; the next you may feel frustrated that you did not come close to reaching your goal. To answer your question, "Yes," you should attempt to teach the year's course of study, but don't feel like a failure if you find that goal impossible some years. **—Clyde Bryan**

Q: *How do you motivate unmotivated learners?*

A: I know a teacher who reached a frustration level that apparently was the last straw for him. He asked all the kids who weren't interested in learning to sit on one side of the room. He then proceeded to teach only the motivated students on the other side of the room. The unmotivated students were given busywork of one kind or another. I don't know how this worked out for him, but I think there are serious questions to be raised regarding this answer to his frustration. The point is that we can all relate to being frustrated with kids we just can't seem to reach.

Be sure your lessons and material are relevant, interesting, and presented in an upbeat fashion. Don't exclude humor, regardless of your students' age level. If you can't turn all of them on, and you can't, don't put yourself on a guilt trip. You're doing all you can do; be encouraged by that. **—Jack Warner**

Q: *How should you evaluate students and their work?*

A: When I began teaching, grading and evaluation were pretty much one and the same. Usually, in intermediate grades through high school, we used letter grading: 90-100% = *A*; 80-89% = *B*; 70-79% = *C*; 60-69% = *D*; and below that = *F*. Clean and simple. Some kids never seem to get better grades than *C*'s or *D*'s, and this might eventually lead to "tracking." In this scenario, the students with lower grades might be perceived to be "dumb" or fair game for a track leading to a steady diet of "easy" classes, things "even they could handle."

Today, many teachers use *authentic assessment* to evaluate their students. (See the glossary for more on buzz words.) Also, teachers are using portfolios for several purposes, one of which is to help you assess a student's progress over a period of time. This can be a help in evaluation. The portfolios can also provide evidence to support a grade, if that is necessary. **—J.W.**

Q: *What do you do about "pullout" kids who miss a lot of class-room time?*

A: These kids are with a resource teacher or specialist for certain times in a day because they've been referred to one of these teachers. Teachers, administrators, specialists, and parents have all agreed that the "pullout" student needs this special attention.

Keep in mind that this student is where he or she should be—not simply "missing" from class. If you are still concerned that these students are losing out on content you want them to learn, talk to their pullout teachers. I've found that they want to know your concerns. They are interested in what your student is missing as well, and they want to work out something agreeable to both of you. **—J.W.**

Q: *How can I meet the needs of each child when my class is so large?*

A: Truth be known, you probably can't meet the needs of every child in your classroom. That doesn't mean, however, that you shouldn't try. If you get to know each child in your class, you certainly have a better chance of helping them. Look through their permanent files and talk with former teachers to give you an idea of any background information. Also, there are many teaching strategies that can lighten your load: parent involvement, peer tutoring, buddy systems, cooperative learning activities, and better use of teaching aides and volunteer help. **—C.B.**

Q: *What should I do when a substitute does not follow my detailed plans?*

A: If your plans are made out in detail and you expect the sub to pick up right where you left off, you'll never be happy with the results. The sub doesn't know where you've been or where you're going with your lessons. There are activities that may flow from day to day, regardless of who's teaching the class; in general, however, I feel it's good to have a good mix of reinforcement or review types of activities planned and ready to use. This is not "busywork," but something that makes sense to you, the only one who knows your class's needs.

As we mentioned in chapter 8, it's a good idea to have a set of emergency lesson plans on hand in the event that you are not able to get any plans to the sub in time. These emergency plans usually include a variety of activities that will make sense on any given day, such as map and globe skills, any number of math concepts, a good piece of literature, and several interesting "sponge" activities. (See chapter 8 for an explanation.) **—J.W.**

Q: *How do I decide whether to retain a child?*

A: If a child is going to be retained, it better be early. Once the student is up into the intermediate grades, I doubt you will get much support in your desire to hold the student back. My experience has been that suggesting to your principal that you have a fourth-grade child who needs to be retained creates a real "hot potato." The obvious question will be "Why wasn't this request made three or four years ago?"

If you do have a legitimate candidate for retention, go through the proper channels to initiate it. Your school probably has an SST (see the glossary at the back of this book), which would likely be your first step of referral. A note of caution: Don't bring up retention to the parents well into the school year, especially if they're under the impression that their youngster is doing at least passing work—I'll show you "hot potato"! **—J.W.**

Q: *Every other year or so I get a student I just flat don't like—I guess you could call it a personality conflict. Is there a solution?*

A: I had to chuckle at this question. Ideally, a teacher should like all students all the time, but this is not an ideal world, is it? Occasionally a "cocklebur" will happen upon the scene. You're an adult and it's your obligation to try to establish rapport—even with the most difficult student. This doesn't mean that you have to be condescending to develop this rapport. It just means that you must try several different ways to develop some type of positive relationship.

If your attempts fail, discuss the issue with your administrator. Explain that you have tried to resolve the situation, nothing has worked, and it could be a personality conflict. Seek the administrator's support in transferring the student to another classroom. Some might question this course of action, but we have known it to be a positive solution for *both* the student and teacher. **—C.B.**

Q: *How do I deal with a class of kids from other cultures who are language-minority kids when I'm not qualified to teach them?*

A: With our ever-expanding numbers of limited-English-proficient children entering our classrooms every year, this is a major problem. Where demographics show large populations of these kids, we have a serious shortage of qualified bilingual teachers. If you are in this situation, hopefully you at least have an aide who speaks the primary language appropriate for your class. Another help for you would be pullout ESL classes on a daily basis. Most language-minority kids need more than this; but again, if the qualified bilingual teachers are not there, you must make the most of what you have.

Here are three typical requirements of states/districts that have bilingual education programs. These requirements say that

- An adequate number of qualified teachers have been assigned to implement the required English-language development (ELD) instruction for each limited-English-proficient (LEP) student.

- An adequate number of qualified teachers have been assigned to implement academic instruction through the primary language for each LEP student.

- Each district provides an adequate in-service training program for existing or future personnel in the bilingual skills necessary to serve each LEP student.

If you teach in a state with a bilingual education program that has similar requirements, you should be getting aide help and training in this program to prepare you for your job. Check with your administrator to find out what is available to you or required of you as an unqualified teacher of LEP kids. I relate completely to your frustrations because I was hired into a classroom of 100 percent Spanish-speaking LEP children. Fortunately for me, my principal and my district were quick to get me a Spanish-speaking aide and set me up in a bilingual training program. Hopefully your district will provide you with the help you need in a very frustrating position. —J.W.

Q: *Why do we keep reinventing the wheel? We know what works so why don't we just get to work and teach?*

A: Here's a question we can relate to! It really seems like we do that in education. Many of us have seen truth in the expression "What goes 'round, comes 'round." When we began our careers, the "unit method" was in. Now we have the Thematic Approach and Integrated Curriculum. What we were doing with our unit teaching was probably a mix of the two. And whole language? My master teacher understood this concept before he knew it had a name. Of course, it didn't then—he didn't know what to call it. It was just "good teaching"! (And maybe you'd have to go a long way to find a better definition for whole language.) New Math? Probably coming back around the bend any minute—in some form.

New teachers and old guys like us are all affected by changes. Ride them out. You know there have to be people out there thinking up all these new methods, approaches, and philosophies. Meanwhile, one thing that will never go out of style is good teaching. Then as things come and go and return with a different name, you can just kind of wink your eye and smile.

Of course, many technological "wheels" are new in recent years, and we must be willing to accept them. There are computer programs that offer exciting alternatives in our class-rooms, and the same can be said for educational television. Take advantage of any technological training offered by your district and you'll find that your teaching will be even more effective. **—J.W.**

Discipline Issues

Q: *What can a first-year teacher do to avoid chronic discipline problems?*

A: It's really important to begin immediately with a good, solid discipline plan that the students thoroughly understand. There are many books on this subject, such as Lee Canter's *Assertive Discipline.* We suggest establishing such a proven plan, one that's workable for you.

This is where Clyde and I part company a bit—not in theory, but in practice. Clyde likes to keep things tight at first and loosen up as he sees fit. I agree in theory, but I've tried this and found it unsuitable to my personality and teaching style. To me, I'm being phony. It works better for me to have the same consistency all year. He says that if students start demonstrating irresponsible behavior later in the year, the mere threat of returning to stricter rule enforcement will usually improve their behavior. **—J.W.**

Q: *How do I handle chronic talking?*

A: This may sound too simplistic, but don't let it get to the "chronic" stage—deal with it quickly. This isn't much help to you if it has already reached that point. Now it's harder, but not as hard as it will be even further down the road. See what your class rules say about excessive talking and what consequences your discipline plan calls for. Then deal with it quickly and firmly to make it easier on yourself for the rest of the school year. **—J.W.**

Q: *One of my penalties for students is having them serve detention. This means I have to monitor them. It works, but it takes my free time. What should I do?*

A: I don't believe in any discipline plan that penalizes the teacher when enforced—you need your time. Some detention plans are supervised on a rotating basis among teachers. This works better, but, in my opinion, is still not right. If you can't work it out with other teachers to share this time, I would suggest two possibilities as alternatives. If it's strictly a punitive thing, handle it by taking away something the student likes to do—some privilege. If you stick with the detention idea and it's for students who have not turned in work, and so on, have them remain after school for a realistic amount of time, but only if they can be in your classroom where you will be working anyway. Then the monitoring process becomes pretty simple. (By the way, when Clyde and I discussed this, we had some very creative alternatives, but we must admit they're probably not legal!) **—J.W.**

Q: *I've been teaching for 21 years and it seems like students have become harder to control. Discipline techniques I used years ago don't work anymore. Is it that I've changed or have the kids changed?*

A: I know exactly what you mean and I'm sure it's because the kids have changed! When I started out, teachers were held in high esteem by society and especially by parents. Parents used to back up the teacher's authority by warning their children of the consequences if they misbehaved at school. This meant that a simple threat such as "I'm afraid I'll have to call your dad if this happens again" put holy fear into the kid! Today, however, many students are being raised in an "X-rated world" by parents who are emotionally troubled and weighed down with the "trappings of the new millennium"; these parents can't or don't teach respect, responsible behavior, or positive self-esteem. This is why our job gets tougher every year, but we shouldn't let it dampen our spirits! These children need us now more than ever. **—J.W.**

Issues with Parents

Q: *How do you deal with a parent who threatens you physically or verbally?*

A: First, try to avoid any situation that might call for a one-on-one confrontation. You usually can sense when there are bad "vibes" between you and a parent; these feelings usually follow some unpleasant experience you have had with one of his or her kids. You can usually avoid this one-on-one thing by calling the parent and talking it out in a confident and courteous tone. Then suggest a meeting for after school a day or so later. You want to deal with a thing like this quickly and get it resolved, but by buying a little time, even one day, chances are that the parent will have cooled down quite a bit. If you still have anxiety after the phone call, you should discuss it with your principal. He or she probably will want to sit in on the conference with you.

If you get caught eyeball-to-eyeball with an irate parent at a school function, such as a parent-teacher conference or athletic event, don't allow yourself to be drawn into an argument or shouting match. In spite of what you might want to say, don't! You will do yourself a favor to let the parent have his or her tirade, and then respond with a somewhat patronizing comment like "I'm really sorry this situation has reached this point. I understand that you're extremely upset and I want to do everything I can to get this taken care of." (You never know what the parent has been smoking or drinking!) If you respond in a calm, cool manner and come across as being sincere, chances are excellent they will pull in their horns. Then you can address the problem in a civil, intelligent manner. If the parent doesn't calm down, separate yourself from the situation—get out of the room and look for help. **—J.W.**

Q: *How do I deal with parents who are happy only if their children get As in every subject?*

A: Nothing less than straight As will do for some parents. They don't seem to understand that their child might not be an A student in any subject, let alone all subjects. They don't understand that a C indicates average, not failure. The results of their unrealistic demands are frequently maladjusted, insecure children with low self-esteem and a feeling of failure. When such parents come on the scene, teachers can diplomatically explain the situation to them, using any published test results as evidence. This is a difficult, if not impossible, task. Conversely, you should appreciate and support parents who have high expectations for their children if those children do have the required ability. —C.B.

Q: *How do you deal with difficult parents?*

A: Parents can be difficult in different ways. Regardless of the type of difficulty, very few problems cannot be talked out if you get right on it. The real hardcore, downright mean parent is a rarity. As with anything else, if a problem is allowed to fester, it will be much more difficult to resolve. Get together with the parents at the first indication of a problem. You'll find that virtually every time you will end up on the "same page." After all, it's the kid's best interest you both have in mind. —J.W.

Q: *Some parents don't seem as interested in their child's education as I am. How can I make parents see the value of education?*

A: Fortunately, most parents are interested in and supportive of their child's education. In attempting to work with parents who appear to be disinterested, you must first determine the situation. If you teach in the primary grades and are working with the oldest child in the family, the parent in question may not know how to be interested. This may sound strange, but some parents, for whatever reason, simply don't know what, if any, role they should play in their child's education. They may think as their parents thought: "We send them to school to learn...end of subject." They simply do not view themselves as members of a team.

Another scenario is the parent who did very poorly in school and feels totally inadequate to help the child. In the upper grades, it is quite possible the child has already exceeded the level of the parent's formal education. In such cases, the parent is simply unable to help the child.

There is also the parent who had repeated bad experiences in school and is fearful of anything relating to school. In this parent's mind, "the less I have to do with school, the better I like it."

Finally, another parent may simply refuse to get involved. This parent may have the ability to help the child, but simply chooses not to. The reasoning goes, "That's what school is for...to teach my kid...that's why I pay taxes...."

With some help and encouragement, you might be able to involve the first three types of parents. You should at least try. In case number four, good luck! **—C.B.**

Q: *How do I deal with overzealous parents who expect me to provide too much work for their children?*

A: This is sort of a reverse twist to what we usually complain about—those who seem disinterested or nonsupportive. I would suggest talking with the parents and determining just what they consider a reasonable amount of work, presumably homework. I would not want to cross over the boundary between teacher expectations and home expectations. Don't impose a standard on them that is not in harmony with their convictions for their child's workload. However, I would bring up a few considerations:

- More is not necessarily better.

- At some point, while piling on more work, you'll reach a line of diminishing returns.

- Student burnout is a realistic possibility.

Most parents will pay attention to a teacher who gives them common-sense suggestions. At times it may not seem so, but I believe teachers are still respected. If a parent still insists on more work, you may have to oblige them, but at least you have done the right thing as a caring teacher and professional. **—J.W.**

Q: *What do I do when parents call me at home about problems with their child?*

A: You can easily and quickly answer some calls; at this point, you should terminate the call in a friendly way. Don't stay on the line to chat—you don't want to encourage calls at home.

If, however, the parent is obviously angry and perhaps abusive, terminate the call as quickly as possible, remaining courteous in what you say and in your tone. Make an appointment with the parent for the next day so the thing doesn't drag on and make you a nervous wreck. You're also buying time for the parent to cool down and for you to collect your thoughts. If the situation seems potentially threatening to you, ask your principal to sit in on the meeting.

Most parents respect a teacher's privacy and will not call you at home. **—J.W.**

Administrative and Coworker Issues

Q: *What do you do about negative or unprofessional teachers?*

A: There's not much you can do about negative or unprofessional teachers whose sole mission is to pull their little clouds of doom and gloom around with them. They find the worst in people and situations. If you want to do combat with them, you can try to "kill them with kindness." You can do this by always smiling at them and being overly pleasant, which really ruins their day! Actually, my suggestion is that you be pleasant to them, but minimize your contact with them. Good teaching requires positive, upbeat individuals. Don't let these negative people drag you down. Give them their due—and move on. **—C.B.**

Q: *Why do administrators insist on boring, repetitious staff meetings?*

A: Most teachers hate faculty meetings, and I'm sure these meetings aren't among the top 10 favorites with administrators, either. They are, however, a necessary evil. These meetings offer an opportunity for the entire faculty to hear the same message at the same place at the same time. The meeting should be a vehicle for communication, offering an exchange of ideas and a means of problem solving. Teachers have an obligation to be on time and attend to business; administrators have an obligation to limit the number of meetings and keep them brief and business-like. **—C.B.**

Q: *What professional organizations should I join and how do I avoid getting caught up in union/district disputes?*

A: Some schools have contracts with unions that represent their teachers. Such arrangements pretty well make one choice for you. There are other organizations you may choose to join, such as local, state, or national reading, math, or science groups. We would encourage you to investigate and join at least one professional organization that interests you.

The second part of the question is more difficult to answer and is really a matter of conscience. Historically, teachers have been disinclined to get involved in union activities; they have preferred to teach. You will no doubt be approached by union representatives requesting you to become actively involved in the local organization. If this happens, ask questions and talk with your colleagues. Don't succumb to pressure; don't allow yourself to be unduly influenced. You have a right to become active in a union; you have a right to be supportive; you have a right to be left alone. The choice is really yours. **—C.B.**

Q: *How do I deal with colleagues who always want to talk shop?*

A: If there's one thing I've discovered for certain about teachers, it's that they must talk about their jobs—usually a problem kid. This may be in the faculty lounge or at a social event such as the staff Christmas party. I have not personally attended any social function with my colleagues where school wasn't the topic most discussed. Try to find a couple of others who share your attitude about this and eat your lunch with them, or sit at their table at the Christmas party. If you're in a situation where you can mingle, mingle your way over to someone willing to talk about something really inspiring—like fly-fishing, golf, herding sheep—anything but school-related stuff! **—J.W.**

Q: *I have questions, but I hate to bother my administrator with them. Any suggestions?*

A: Don't assume that your administrator doesn't have time for your questions. He or she may welcome them. Some administrators find it helps them keep abreast of happenings in the classroom and gives them an opportunity to discuss issues and get opinions from staff members.

You must "read" your administrator carefully. If you sense he or she is bothered by your questions, seek out colleagues who are "in the know." They can usually answer most questions. **—C.B.**

Q: *Why don't we get rid of some of the "glitz" in education (too many administrators, not enough people directly involved with the children)?*

A: We share your philosophy regarding spending: The closer to the pupils the money is spent, the more efficient its use. Most administrators, like most teachers, are sincere, hardworking people. The problems occur when bureaucracies are created over a period of time to administer special government pro- grams. Although these programs benefit exceptional and under- achieving students, for example, they do require a lot of admin- istrative time for extensive record-keeping and monitoring in order to stay in compliance with government mandates and regulations. **—C.B.**

Q: *I know I'm supposed to report any signs of sexual abuse, so what do I do if one parent confides in me that another family member is sexually abusing one of my students? Do I honor that confidentiality?*

A: You probably will be required to attend an in-service on this subject, at which you will be told about your legal responsibili- ties to report any suspected child neglect or abuse. You can make this report anonymously since the laws in most states require that the name of the person reporting the abuse be kept confidential. In a situation like the one you have described, as soon as you sense that a parent (or anyone) is starting to divulge this type of information, warn that person that you are **required by law** to report any suspicions of sexual abuse. If the parent asks you to keep this information confidential, explain that you **cannot!** A teacher doesn't fall under "attorney-client confidenti- ality" laws, for example, and so you must always report any type of abuse **immediately** to your principal, the school nurse, or directly to the proper government agency. **—J.W.**

Personal Issues

Q: *What advice would you give a new member on your staff?*

A: Ask for help from colleagues. Most teachers are teachers because they like to help people. Because you are a person, you qualify! Don't get discouraged when you feel overwhelmed. Teaching is a job with no end. If you choose to work until the job is "done," give your landlord notice: You'll no longer need a place to stay, and you'll need the rent money to pay the Domino's Pizza driver who brings your meals to school! Find a balance between your professional life and personal life. **—C.B.**

Q: *If I'm enjoying my classroom position, should I consider "moving up" to a position of higher authority?*

A: This is a question most, if not all, teachers wrestle with at some time in their careers. The answer depends on the individual. If you are happy teaching (most of the time!) and sincerely enjoy your daily contact with students, there really is no reason to move up. If, on the other hand, you start to become restless and want to try something else in education, you need to do a lot of talking with people who currently hold positions like those that interest you. You should also read extensively and even take a related college course or two. You might "job shadow" during times that do not conflict with your teaching duties. You also need to assess your own skills and personality.

Points to consider: "Up" is not always "better." Success in the classroom does not ensure success as an administrator. More than one administrator has realized after the fact that he or she made a mistake leaving the classroom. Whatever your decision, I strongly suggest you do your homework before making it. **—C.B.**

Q: *How do I find time for everything every day?*

A: You won't find time to do "everything every day" as long as there are only 24 hours in a day. Except for the end of the school year, teaching is one of those professions that has no definable end. Teachers have a habit of thinking there is always something else that needs to be accomplished. Look at the givens: You have from 25 to 35 students and five to seven subjects to teach in five or six time slots. Obviously, you can't do everything every day. The key is good planning, good evaluation, and reasonable expectations for the children and yourself. **—C.B.**

Q: *Is it my imagination, or is teaching more stressful than it used to be?*

A: *Life* is more stressful today than it used to be. It follows that a profession that has always been a bit stressful would also have increased stress. Stress in a teacher's life has many causes: the decline of family structure, increasing class sizes, single-parent families, both parents working, changing social values, students questioning authority, limited resources...the list seems endless.

These complex social and financial problems have no easy solutions. Dwelling on them simply brings about more stress. The best advice we can offer is this: We are in a people-oriented business, and basically, in spite of the times, people have not changed that much. You realize this when you sit and talk with them person-to-person. They still have a strong desire to succeed—and who is in a better position to help them do that than you? **—C.B.**

Q: *Somehow I thought teaching would be a profession with a real team spirit, but it's turned into a lonely job. Is it just me, or is this common?*

A: Teaching is a profession with real team spirit—most of the time. On occasion it can be lonely, depending in part on you and in part on the staff with whom you work. It's easy to get in the habit of "living" in your classroom. Sometimes it is just easier to spend recess or lunch hour at your desk rather than journey to the staff room. We know of one teacher who never went to the staff room once during his first year of teaching. In some cases, you might work on a staff that has a significant age difference from you and you might have trouble relating to them.

Like classes of students, teaching staffs have composite personalities. Some are friendly and outgoing, making new teachers feel welcome. The other extreme is a staff where members pretty well keep to themselves and just do their jobs. They aren't hostile, but they are not particularly friendly, either. Fortunately, most staffs tend to be like the former.

It is important that you be able to socialize with your staff. If the staff tends to be friendly, count yourself lucky. If the staff is not friendly, you have to make an effort to become acquainted. If, as the year progresses, things are not going well with the staff and you are unhappy, you should consider changing schools. You need to be able to look forward to going to work each day. Working with an upbeat, friendly staff helps. **—C.B.**

Q: *Since I started teaching I seem to get sick more often than before. What can I do to keep from picking up colds and flu from my students?*

A: As if teaching isn't stressful enough, we also have to put up with the occupational hazard of being exposed to bacterial infections, viruses, chickenpox, lice, ringworm, and whatever else might be floating around our classrooms each day. Unfortunately, you will probably pick up the most cold and flu bugs during your first year or two of teaching, which are already the most difficult years you'll ever have to face! Our best advice is to take every preventative measure you can, including these:

- Take a daily vitamin tablet, along with extra vitamin C.

- Wash your hands frequently during the day; keep a bar of disinfectant soap handy (such as Dial).

- Try not to touch your nose, mouth, and eyes during the day.

- Get a flu shot as soon as possible each year.

- Eat well-balanced meals.

- Get plenty of exercise.

- Get plenty of sleep.

- Bring a can of Lysol spray to school; use it around your desk, on doorknobs, on cabinet handles, on the pencil sharpener, on the telephone receiver, and so on. Also, spray daily around the sink and water fountain.

- Drink lots of water.

- Send a sick child to the school nurse. (Ask her to call the parent to come pick up any child who is sick with flu or a cold!) Unfortunately, many parents send their sick children to school because they can't afford child-care expenses.

- Take frequent bathroom breaks to prevent bladder and kidney infections. Teachers are particularly susceptible to these infections because they get stuck in the classroom with few breaks. Arrange with the closest teacher to watch each other's classes long enough for each of you to keep your bladders empty!

Just remember that the first year or two are the worst. After several years in the classroom, you'll find that your resistance builds up to the point where you aren't sick as much.
–J.W. and C.B.

Note: If you still have unanswered questions, see www.teachers.net, which offers teachers a chance to vent, as well as receive answers to their questions. Also, see "Support Groups" in the appendix.

Chapter 13

"I Think I Can... I Think I Can..."

We hope our "inside secrets" have been encouraging. Our goal has been to save you years of frustrating trial and error in your teaching career. We want you to feel comfortable with the staff at your school, be familiar with the buzz words, and get a "leg up" on rapport with your students and their parents. We've also suggested shortcuts for decorating and supplying your classroom, along with insider info on extracurriculars.

The number one reason why teachers quit the profession is their inability to control their classrooms, so we tackled this tough problem with tried-and-true methods that may save your sanity in your first years of teaching. High stress and lack of time management also cause teacher burnout, but perhaps you can conquer these two villains by using a few of our ideas.

By recognizing the fact that you'll never get "done"–it's the nature of the profession–we hope you'll keep your job in perspective! Learning to separate your personal and professional lives is the key. You can be a devoted, conscientious teacher and still have time to relax with your family!

Yes, it's a busy, complicated profession, but, in our opinion, it's the noblest of all. Think back over your school experience. Certain teachers stand out. Those teachers made a difference in people's lives. Strive to become such a teacher. Take pride in your teaching career and remember that each and every day you show even one student that you care, you've had a good day!

After many years of teaching, some of your students will drift back for a visit, or you will bump into them in a store. They'll say things like "You were the best teacher I ever had," or "You taught me how to think, how to study," or "You always made me feel good about myself—thank you." Your rewards will come, although you may not see them on a daily basis. You need only to believe in the sanctity of your profession, realize the value of each student entrusted to you, and have faith in yourself.

Remember: Teaching is a marathon, not a sprint!

All Those Buzz Words!

As you start out on the teaching staff, you may be overwhelmed with hundreds of acronyms and strange-sounding terms and phrases that are apparently necessary to educators. These "buzz words" of the profession often can be intimidating, especially if it seems that those around you know what they mean and you don't. Some of these words should be familiar to you from your university courses; others will be foreign to your ears. In fact, you may wonder how you ever graduated without knowing more of these terms. Have no fear—they are much less frightening than they seem at first.

One thing you'll have to get used to in this profession is that educators often have a tough time agreeing on the definition and interpretation of many of the buzz words they use. At a recent staff meeting of some two dozen teachers, the term *whole language* came up and it quickly became apparent that all were not "on the same page" as to its meaning.

Many of these buzz words are thrown around so loosely that it's no wonder they become confusing at times. One word of caution: When using this teacher jargon around parents or those outside the teaching profession, explain any acronyms or terms you use in your conversation. Try putting these terms into layman's language; parents especially appreciate the effort.

Although these buzz words will descend on you in random order, we have listed them alphabetically for easy reference.

ADA (Average Daily Attendance)

A count of students in attendance or with excused absences. The ADA determines the amount of state funding districts receive.

Advisory Council

A group of parents, community members, and school employees involved in the planning and evaluation of educational programs at the school.

AFDC (Aid to Families with Dependent Children)

The federally funded welfare program for families whose income is below the poverty level. The AFDC count is the primary factor in determining a district's entitlement for ESEA Chapter 1 funding (see "ESEA Chapter 1," below).

Assertive Discipline

A behavior-management plan for the classroom that lets the students know the teacher's behavioral expectations. Students receive positive recognition when they choose to follow the class rules, and face negative consequences when they misbehave or choose not to follow the class rules.

At-Risk Students

Students who are low-achieving because of poor home environment, low self-image, or low ability. These students, if left to their own motivation, seldom graduate from high school.

Auditory, Visual, and Kinesthetic Learners

Auditory learners generally learn best through verbal instructions. *Visual learners* generally learn most easily by seeing; that is, by watching demonstrations. *Kinesthetic learners* generally learn best by doing; this means direct involvement with hands-on activities.

Authentic Assessment

A method of creative assessment and evidence of students' work. Some examples of this type of assessment are art projects, journals, portfolios, drama and oral presentations, discussions of literature, written reports, and field trip follow-up activities.

Behavior Modification

The learning theory that rewards good behavior and punishes bad behavior, with the idea that a student's behavior will eventually change as a result, becoming more good than bad.

Bilingual Education

Educational services provided to limited-English-proficient (LEP) students (see "LEP [limited-English-proficient]," below). Bilingual education provides instruction to students in their primary language and helps them develop English skills.

Bloom's Taxonomy

The classification system designating a hierarchy of six levels of cognitive skills. These skills are listed below in order from most concrete to most abstract:

1. Knowledge

2. Comprehension

3. Application

4. Analysis

5. Synthesis

6. Evaluation

Capital Outlay

Program costs related to equipment and facilities.

Categorical Programs

Federal and state-authorized programs in which funds must be used for a specific purpose.

CD-ROM

Here's a term that has started buzzing around teachers' lounges and in-services in the last several years. *CD* means *compact disk* and *ROM* means *read-only memory*. The disks themselves are similar to those you use on your musical CD player; however, instead of songs and symphonies, these CDs are loaded with data. To use one of these CDs, you need a CD-ROM drive attached to your computer (about $280). You insert a CD into this drive and your computer can read the data off the ROM. One disk can hold the equivalent of 2,000 full-length novels of 75,000 words each (600,000 double-spaced, typewritten pages). This means that if you have 20 CDs sitting on top of your desk, they take up a space 8½ inches wide, 5 inches deep, and 5 inches high, but contain 12 million pages of information! CD-ROM is not only the buzz word of the future, but terrific technology that is here today (and affordable, too).

Classified Personnel

Non-certificated employees, including teaching aides, secretaries, and custodians (who are not required to have special teaching credentials).

Compensatory Education

Supplemental instruction and support services provided by categorical funding (see "Categorical Programs," above) to children identified as educationally disadvantaged (see "EDY [Educationally Disadvantaged Youth]," below).

Cooperative Learning

Learning that takes place among students in small groups. The structure of the classroom is changed so that instead of students listening only to the teacher, they may interact in small groups (typically three to six students) and learn from each other. Cooperative learning works well with language-minority children because it allows them to learn at their own pace; it allows them to understand a concept before having to demonstrate oral and written skills; and it keeps their anxieties to a minimum because of the smaller, less-threatening grouping.

Core Curriculum

A district's basic course of study for all students.

Cross-Age Tutor

An older student who helps a younger student. This can be accomplished within the classroom or between classrooms or schools.

Cross-Culture

With increasing numbers of children entering our classrooms from other cultures, it's essential that we have awareness of and respect for these cultural differences. Many activities can be used throughout the year to achieve a truly cross-cultural classroom, in addition to a day-to-day sensitivity to these children and their native cultures. An example of a typical activity might be the observance of a special holiday of one culture, other than American, that is represented in your classroom.

Cumulative Folder

A folder, usually kept in the school office, containing a cumulative record of each student's test results, personal history, health records, family background, who to contact in case of emergency, personal characteristics, comments from past teachers, social skills, past peer relationships, copies of all report cards from all schools attended, results of any special-education testing, past referrals to resource teachers, and parent consent forms. This folder follows the student from grade to grade and school to school.

EDY (Educationally Disadvantaged Youth)

A federal designation for students whose educational attainment is below the level appropriate for children their age, identified by scores on nationally standardized tests.

ELD (English Language Development)

Specialized English instruction designed for students whose primary language (or L-1) is something other than English. The instructional techniques, materials used, and approaches are directed toward communicative competence and academic achievement in English.

EO (English Only)

A student whose primary language is English as indicated by the Home Language Survey; or indicating a classroom for students whose L-1 is English.

ERIC

The Educational Resources Information Center, sponsored by the U.S. Department of Education. This is an excellent source of educational research. ERIC's Web address is www.accesseric.org.

ESEA Chapter 1

Part of the Elementary and Secondary Education Act of 1988 that provides supplemental federal financial assistance to school districts to meet the instructional needs of educationally disadvantaged students (see "EDY," above).

ESEA Chapter 2

Part of the Elementary and Secondary Education Act of 1988 that provides supplemental federal financial assistance to school districts for the purpose of improving elementary and secondary education with seven focus areas.

ESL (English as a Second Language)

A component of the base curriculum of an LEP (limited-English-proficient) student, involving the teaching of English-language proficiency to students whose primary language is something other than English.

Evaluation (Teacher)

The evaluation of a teacher's performance according to the policies of the school district. An evaluation can be done by a designated administrator at various times during the school year; generally, new teachers are evaluated more frequently than experienced teachers.

FEP (Fluent-English Proficient)

A student whose primary language is not English and who has shown English academic language proficiency through the process of reclassification (see "Reclassification/ Redesignation," below).

Free Appropriate Public Education

One of the key requirements of Public Law 94-142, which requires an educational program for all children without cost to parents.

Hands-on

The actual "doing," as opposed to theory or understanding through reading or writing about something. The use of manipulatives and/or participating physically in a science experiment, such as making an electric circuit with wires, batteries, and a bell or light bulb.

HLS (Home Language Survey)

A form completed by a parent or guardian when the student is enrolled in a public school, determining the student's primary language. This form may be called something else in your state.

Holistic Scoring/Rubric Scoring Guide

This is a valid and reliable way to evaluate a student's work, particularly a piece of written work. The work is scored as a whole, or as a single overall impression, rather than by breaking it down into its various parts. The scorer rates the work on a numerical scale, commonly called the *Rubric* or *Scoring Guide*. This Rubric identifies high, middle, and low quality levels of proficiency for each piece of work being scored. A number designation is given to that work, representing its grade relative to the established criteria of the Rubric.

Hyperactivity

Behavior demonstrated by a student who is excessively or abnormally active.

IEP (Individualized Education Program)

A component of Public Law 94-142 (see "Free Appropriate Public Education," above) that requires a written plan of instruction for each child who receives special services.

In-Services

Teacher training sessions in the form of classes, lectures, or seminars offered by schools or school districts. These sessions teach certain academic and social concepts, such as "How to Instill Self-Esteem in Your Students."

Integrated Curriculum

Pulling all the curriculum into one unit of study or one theme. (See "Thematic Approach," below.)

Internal and External Motivation

Ways that a student can be motivated to learn. *Internal motivation* comes from within the student, driven by curiosity and the desire to "figure it out." *External motivation* comes from other people in the student's life, such as parents, teachers, and peers.

L-1 (Primary Language)

The language that was first learned by the student or is spoken in the student's home, as indicated on the Home Language Survey.

L-2 (Secondary Language)

If English is the second language or language of acquisition, it is considered the student's *L-2.*

LDS (Language Development Specialist)

A certificated teacher trained to provide English as a Second Language instruction to limited-English-proficient students.

LEA (Language Experience Approach)

A teaching approach characterized by student activity and creativity. One example might be a class cooking a food dish. After completion of the activity, the teacher uses it as the basis for further language-development activities.

Learning Centers

Areas in the classroom designated for the study of specific subjects. Also known as *Interest Centers.* (For more information, see chapter 6, "The Classroom Environment.")

Least Restrictive Educational Environment

A concept expressed by the courts in the 1970s, in essence saying that disabled persons should be educated in the best possible environment. This led to the idea of "mainstreaming" (see "Mainstreaming," below).

LEP (limited-English-proficient)

A student whose primary language is other than English and who has not been reclassified. This student has not developed English academic language skills in listening, speaking, reading, and writing at a level substantially equivalent to students of the same grade or age whose primary language is English.

Mainstreaming

Officially moving a student from a bilingual or special-education class into a regular classroom.

Mentor Teacher

An exemplary teacher selected to share expertise and support with colleagues on the staff. New teachers are often assigned a mentor teacher.

Migrant Education

A federally funded categorical program to provide supplemental health and education services to students whose families move frequently because of jobs related to agriculture or fishing.

Modeling

Demonstrating exactly what the student is to do by providing a perfect example. A common formula for modeling is the following:

1. I do it.

2. I do it; you help me.

3. You do it; I help you.

4. You do it.

Multicultural Curriculum

A curriculum whereby children study the history and culture of different ethnic groups. This curriculum teaches them to appreciate the diversity of our population and is intended to reduce prejudice.

NEA

The National Education Association, a national organization of teachers that provides legislative lobbying, services, and support for teachers, including the monthly *NEA TODAY* publication. Note: There are also state and local teachers' organizations to which teachers may belong.

NEA Online

An electronic network offered to NEA members via the Internet, whereby teachers can share insights with their colleagues and download useful information to their home computers. This service is available to NEA members for a modest monthly fee.

Networking

A form of communication between teachers in a school or school district who have similar problems peculiar to a certain subject or grade level. Usually the teachers meet, exchange phone numbers, and share support and helpful information.

Pedagogy

The art or profession of teaching.

Peer Tutoring

Teammates help each other learn some content area of the curriculum or practice a skill together, such as a basic math fact.

Portfolios

Folders or files that keep a wide variety of work samples for each individual student. These samples can provide comparisons of a student's work over a period of time, from several months to several years. This comparison can help determine the student's progress and achievement. Many teachers encourage students to become involved in selecting work samples to go into the portfolios. Portfolios can be used to provide evidence and support for grades given.

Prep Period

Also called *prep time,* this is a time of day designated by the school district to be used by teachers for preparation and planning lessons, correcting papers, and so on. With diminishing budgets, many districts can no longer afford to offer this period to their teachers.

Public Law 94-142

This is the Education for All Handicapped Children Act passed by Congress in 1975, which guarantees a free appropriate education to school-aged handicapped children.

Pullout Program

A program for students with identified learning disabilities who are pulled out of regular classrooms for special help from a qualified teacher.

Reclassification/Redesignation

A process whereby a student is officially reclassified from LEP (limited-English-proficient) to FEP (fluent-English-proficient). This is done through testing established by the school district, in accordance with state standards. The student may then be mainstreamed into an EO (English Only) classroom after the reclassification has been made.

SAC (School Advisory Council)

A committee made up of parents and staff members, which is required for the school's implementation of compensatory education programs; also the committee for ESEA Chapter 1 programs.

SDC (Special Day Class)

A self-contained class or center that offers full-time instruction to children whose handicaps prevent them from participating in a regular class.

Sex Equity

The elimination of sexual stereotyping when teaching or communicating. For example, you may want to avoid wording such as, "the construction worker…he" or "the nurse…she."

Shared Teaching

A situation in which two teachers share the responsibilities of teaching one class. The arrangement may be tailored in a variety of ways. For example, Teacher A works three days a week and Teacher B works two, or Teacher A works mornings and Teacher B works afternoons.

Sheltered English

A method of teaching subject matter to limited-English-proficient (LEP) students in their language of acquisition (L-2). The teacher's use of visuals, graphics, manipulatives, appropriate body language, and facial expressions are some of the ways to make the subject matter more comprehendible for the LEP student. The vocabulary should be kept in context, not in isolated lists, and teaching should proceed from the concrete to the abstract.

Specials

A term for nonacademic subjects, such as art, music, and P.E. Many school districts provide teachers who teach only specials, thus relieving the classroom teacher for prep periods.

Split Class

Two or more grade levels in one class; also known as a *combination class*.

SST (Student Study Team)

A group that meets in the local school to determine a child's educational needs and individualized education program. The group is made up of the school principal (or other administrator), teachers or specialists, parents, and others as necessary.

Standardized Testing

An achievement test given to a student to measure academic progress; this test uses nationalized norms.

Temps or Portables

Portable or modular buildings brought onto school grounds to be used as additional temporary classrooms until permanent classrooms can be built. Note: We've noticed that "temps" have a way of becoming "perms."

Tenure

A term used to describe the permanent status reached by a teacher within a school district, as opposed to probationary or nontenured status.

Thematic Approach

Also called *thematic teaching,* this is the development of all or most subject area content around a specific theme. For example, if your theme is "Changes in the World Around Us," your lessons would be adapted to the concept of change, regardless of the curriculum area.

Time-Out

A method of discipline whereby a student is sent to a designated spot in the classroom or school for a specified length of time, providing a time-out for the student (and teacher, too, on occasion).

Title VII ESEA (Elementary and Secondary Education Act, 1986)

A federal measure that provides assistance to local agencies. Funds support efforts being made to provide LEP students with an equal educational opportunity.

TPR (Total Physical Response)

An approach to second language acquisition that emphasizes physical response from the student. Commands such as "stand up," "sit down," and "put your hand on your head" are examples of TPR. This approach focuses more on interesting content than on form or grammar.

Tracking

Tracking is a system whereby students are grouped according to their perceived academic ability. This concept is becoming passé, however, and the current trend is to "untrack" students.

Whole Language

Whole language is a philosophy, a set of beliefs; not a single approach to teaching. Whole language is characterized by children learning naturally, with the learning progressing from whole to part. This literature-rich environment places an emphasis on the language's use and meaning. Skills are not taught in an isolated, sequential way, but in the context of what's going on in the classroom.

Note: See "Organizations" and "Resources" in the appendix for Web sites that will help you stay abreast of the latest buzz words.

Helpful Web Sites for Teachers

Organizations

American Federation of Teachers
`www.aft.org`

A labor organization for teachers; includes education-related articles.

Association of Teacher Educators
`www.edweek.org/context/orgs/ate.htm`

A national membership organization founded in 1920.

Education Week on the Web
`www.edweek.org`

Education news–keeps up with what's new and exciting in education.

Educational Resources Information Center (ERIC)
`www.accesseric.org/home.html`

Has virtually all significant documents related to any aspect of education.

National Center for Education Statistics
`www.nces.ed.gov`

The Web site for the primary federal agency for collecting and analyzing data related to education in the United States and other nations.

National Education Association
www.nea.org

Resources and information about school reform and newsgroups for K–12 education.

National PTA
www.pta.org

Learn more about the history, services, and initiatives of the national parent-teacher volunteer organization. The site has events and bulletin boards.

U.S. Department of Education
www.ed.gov

Information and research from the government agency that oversees education.

Word Games and Art
www.edgamesandart.com/ptalinks.html

Links to parent-teacher associations; organizations for parents, teachers, and early-childhood educators.

Resources

Academic Software
www.academicsoftwareusa.com

The latest academic software at competitive prices.

Arizona State Public Information Network: Teacher Resources
http://aspin.asu.edu/~casey/webresources/

Lesson plans, curricula, and classroom ideas.

AskERIC
http://ericir.syr.edu

Over 3,000 resources compiled in response to teachers' questions to ERIC (the Educational Resources Information Center).

Ball Elementary (IL): Teacher Resources
http://bes.bcsd.k12.il.us/teach.htm

New ideas, lesson plans, additional resources on any topic, and links for teachers.

The BIG PAGES of Teacher Resource Sites
www.mts.net/~jgreenco/teacher.html

Recommended general teaching sites.

Birch Lane School (CA): Teacher Resources
http://birchlane.davis.ca.us/webstuff/teach.htm

A comprehensive listing of online lessons, activities, projects, resources, references, and tools for teachers.

Continental Press
www.continentalpress.com

Publisher of supplemental education materials.

Creative Publications
www.creativepublications.com

A developer and publisher of supplemental products for math education.

Dorseyville Middle School (PA): Links for Music Teachers
www.fcasd.edu/schools/dms/tmu.htm

Essential links for music education.

Educational Insights
www.educationalinsights.com

Educational toys and games.

EdWeb
http://edweb.gsn.org

Helpful information for educators regarding technology and school reform.

Encarta Schoolhouse

www.encarta.msn.com/Schoolhouse

Online resources designed for educators in grades 7–12. Features Microsoft reference facts and links.

The Explorer

http://explorer.scrtec.org

Math and science for K–12.

Free Lesson Plans

www.lessonplanspage.com

Curriculum materials.

Glenbrook North (IL) Mathematics Department Teacher Resources

www.glenbrook.k12.il.us/gbnmath/TR.html

Math-related teacher resources and lesson plans.

Internet Resources for Teacher Librarians: Teacher Development

www3.sympatico.ca/rbudding/tlresources/tchrdevt.htm

Provides teachers with direct source materials, lesson plans, and classroom activities.

Lakeshore Learning Materials

www.lakeshorelearning.com

Educational supplies and materials for early childhood and grades 1–3.

Los Angeles County Office of Education: Conferences and Events

http://teams.lacoe.edu/documentation/news/conferences.html

Education conferences.

Meridian Joint School District (ID): Links for Teachers
www.sd02.k12.id.us/103/lteach.htm

Links for teachers that include resources, curriculum ideas, and guides to other Internet sites.

myteacher.net: Teacher Links
http://myteacher.net/edresources/teacher.html

Teacher links for resources, products, supplies, and organizations.

The National Science Foundation
www.nsf.gov

An independent U.S. government agency responsible for promoting science and engineering through programs that invest over $3.3 billion per year in almost 20,000 research and education projects in science and engineering.

Northern Lebanon (PA) School District: Web Links for Students and Teachers
www.norleb.k12.pa.us/documents/links.htm

Helpful Internet links for math, science, social studies, language arts, and miscellaneous other topics.

PE Central
http://pe.central.vt.edu

Information for health and physical education teachers.

Perfection Learning
www.perfectionlearning.com

A leading publisher of teacher and student curriculum materials for grades pre-K–12.

ProTeacher
www.proteacher.com

Web directory for elementary-school teachers in grades pre-K–6. Early-childhood, elementary, and middle-school lesson plans, activities, teaching ideas, and resources on the Internet.

Scholastic Professional Books
http://teacher.scholastic.com/index.htm

Lesson plans, reproducibles, resources, authors and books, online activities, news, research tools, book and software clubs, and reading programs.

Teaching Resource Center
www.trcabc.com/teaching_resource_materials/
sch_supls.html

Resource materials and school supplies at better prices.

Teachers.Net
www.teachers.net

Teacher resources, reference tools, forums, and more.

Teacher Support Software
www.tssoftware.com

An educational software publisher.

United Art and Education Supply Co.
www.unitednow.com

Web site for a large national school-supply chain.

Support Groups

Links2Go: K12 Newsgroups
www.links2go.com/more/www.liszt.com/news/k12

Teacher newsgroups; links to topics related to K–12 teaching.

SchoolNotes.com
www.schoolnotes.com

Links educators to their communities by enabling them to post notes and homework for their students.

Teacher Talk Home Page
http://education.indiana.edu/cas/tt/tthmpg.html

A publication for preservice and secondary-education teachers, sponsored by the Indiana University School of Education.

Teachers.Net
www.teachers.net

Helpful information for those in the teaching profession, plus the chance to ask questions, vent, and so on.

Violence Prevention

Bureau of Justice Statistics
www.ojp.usdoj.gov/bjs/abstract/iscs00.htm

Indicators of School Crime and Safety, 2000.

Center for the Study and Prevention of Violence, University of Colorado, Boulder
www.colorado.edu/cspv/

An organization that provides informed assistance to groups committed to understanding and preventing violence.

The Denver Post Online
www.denverpost.com/news/shotmain.htm

Details of the Columbine tragedy.

Early Warning, Timely Response: A Guide to Safe Schools
www.ed.gov/offices/OSERS/OSEP/earlywrn.html

An online violence-prevention guide based on the work of an independent panel of experts in the fields of education, law enforcement, and mental health. Much of the research was funded by federal offices.

Keep Schools Safe
www.keepschoolssafe.org

A collection of resources to help make schools safer and help prevent violence.

National Crime Prevention Council: Stopping School Violence
www.ncpc.org/2schvio.htm

Background and prevention information on this prevalent issue; links to resources.

National Criminal Justice Reference Service
http://www.ncjrs.org/works

Preventing Crime: What Works, What Doesn't, What's Promising.

National Resource Center for Safe Schools:
The SafetyZone
www.safetyzone.org

The National Resource Center for Safe Schools works with schools, communities, state and local education agencies, and other concerned individuals and agencies to create safe learning environments and prevent school violence.

The Network of Violence Prevention Practitioners
www2.edc.org/nvpp

Provides practitioners with an increasingly global forum for exchanging information and experiences from the field, opportunities for professional development, and dialogue between practitioners, researchers, evaluators, and policy-makers to improve violence prevention in our communities.

Partnerships Against Violence Network
www.pavnet.org

A "virtual library" of information about violence and youth-at-risk, representing data from seven different federal agencies.

Bibliography

Albert, L. *A Teacher's Guide to Cooperative Discipline:* American Guidance Service, 1996.

Appleman, D. and McClear, J. *Teacher, the Children Are Here:* Scott, Foresman and Company, 1991.

Bauer, A.M. *Managing Classrooms to Facilitate Learning:* Prentice Hall, 1990.

Bullough, R.V., Jr. *First-Year Teacher: A Case Study:* Teachers College Press, 1989.

Cangelosi, J.S. *Cooperation in the Classroom: Students and Teachers Together:* NEA Professional Library, 1989.

Canter, L. and Canter, M. *Assertive Discipline:* Canter and Associates, 1986.

Charles, C.M. *Building Classroom Discipline: From Models to Practice:* Longman, 1989.

Cherry, Clare. *Please Don't Sit on the Kids: Alternatives to Punitive Discipline:* Pitman Learning, 1982.

Collins, C. *Time Management for Teachers:* Parker Publishing, 1987.

Cotton, D.H. *Stress Management:* Brunner/Mazel, 1993.

Curwin, R.L. and Mendier, A.N. *Discipline with Dignity:* Association for Supervision and Curriculum Development, 1999.

Dreikurs, R.; Grunwald, B.; and Pepper, R. *Maintaining Sanity in the Classroom,* 2nd ed.: Harper and Row, 1998.

Duke, D.L. and Meckel, A.M. *Teacher's Guide to Classroom Management:* Random House, 1984.

Englander, M.E. *Strategies for Classroom Discipline:* Praeger, 1986.

Everly, G.S. *A Clinical Guide to the Treatment of the Human Stress Response:* Plenum Press, 1989.

Evertson, C.M.; Emmer, E.T.; Clements, B.S.; Sanford, J.P.; and Worsham, M.E. *Classroom Management for Elementary Teachers:* Prentice Hall, 1994.

Freeman, Y.S. and Freeman, D.E. *Whole Language:* Heinemann Educational Books, Inc., 1992.

Goleman, D. and Gurin, J. *Mind Body Medicine:* Consumer Reports Books, 1993.

Greenburg, J.S. *Comprehensive Stress Management:* William C. Brown Communications, 1999.

Jackson, P.W. *Life in Classrooms:* Teachers College Press, 1990.

Johns, E.A.; MacNaughton, R.H.; and Karabinus, N.G. *School Discipline Guidebook: Theory into Practice:* Allyn and Bacon, 1989.

Jones, F.H. *Positive Classroom Discipline:* McGraw-Hill, 1987.

Jones, V.E. and Jones, L.S. *Comprehensive Classroom Management: Creating Communities of Support and Solving Problems:* Allyn and Bacon, 2000.

Kane, R.R. *The First Year of Teaching: Real World Stories from America's Schools:* Walker, 1997.

Keating, B.; Pickering, M.; Slack, B.; and White, J. *A Guide to Positive Discipline: Helping Students Make Responsible Choices:* Allyn and Bacon, 1990.

Lemlach, J.K. *Classroom Management: Methods and Techniques for Elementary and Secondary Teachers,* Second Edition: Longman, 1991.

Levin, J. and Nola, J.E. *Principles of Classroom Management: A Hierarchical Approach:* Prentice Hall, 1995.

Malm, K. *Behavior Management in K–6 Classrooms:* NEA Professional Library, 1991.

Martin, R.J. *Teaching Through Encouragement: Techniques to Help Students Learn:* Prentice Hall, 1980.

Purkey, W.W. and Stanley, P.H. *Invitational Teaching, Learning, and Living:* NEA Professional Library, 1989.

Reyes, R. *The Ten Commandments for Teaching:* NEA Professional Library, 1991.

Rivers, L.W. *The Disruptive Student and the Teacher:* NEA Professional Library, 1977.

Schell, L.M. and Burden, Paul. *Countdown to the First Day of School:* NEA Professional Library, 1992.

Seeman, H. *Preventing Classroom Discipline Problems: A Guide for Educators:* Technomic Publishing, 2000.

Sprick, R.S. *Discipline in the Secondary Classroom: A Problem-by-Problem Survival Guide:* Center for Applied Research in Education, 1985.

Steere, B.F. *Becoming an Effective Classroom Manager: A Resource for Teachers:* State University of New York Press, 1988.

Walker, J.E. and Shay, T.M. *Behavior Management: A Practical Approach for Educators,* Fifth Edition: Macmillan, 1984.

Williamson, B. *Classroom Management: A Guidebook for Success:* Dynamic Teaching, 1992.

Williamson, B. *101 Ways to Put Pizzazz into Your Teaching:* Dynamic Teaching, 1991.

Index